P9-AGM-466

DEAN OF FACULTY

E 318

The Cognition Workbook

Essays, Demonstrations, & Explorations

The Cognition Workbook

Essays, Demonstrations, & Explorations

Daniel Reisberg

Reed College

W. W. Norton & Company
New York • London

W. W. Norton & Company has been independent since its founding in 1923, when William Warder Norton and Mary D. Herter Norton first published lectures delivered at the People's Institute, the adult education division of New York City's Cooper Union. The firm soon expanded its program beyond the Institute, publishing books by celebrated academics from America and abroad. By midcentury, the two major pillars of Norton's publishing program—trade books and college texts—were firmly established. In the 1950s, the Norton family transferred control of the company to its employees, and today—with a staff of four hundred and a comparable number of trade, college, and professional titles published each year—W. W. Norton & Company stands as the largest and oldest publishing house owned wholly by its employees.

Copyright © 2010 by W. W. Norton & Company, Inc.

All rights reserved

Printed in the United States of America

Editor: Sheri L. Snavely

Editorial assistant: Wamiq Jawaid

Production editors: Rebecca A. Homiski and Sarah Mann

Production manager: Ben Reynolds

Copyeditor: Alice Vigliani

Design: Lisa Buckley, Rebecca A. Homiski, and Matrix Publishing Services

Composition: Matrix Publishing Services

Manufacturing: R. R. Donnelley—Harrisonburg South

ISBN: 978-0-393-93295-9

W. W. Norton & Company, Inc., 500 Fifth Avenue, New York, NY 10110

www.wwnorton.com

W. W. Norton & Company Ltd., Castle House, 75/76 Wells Street, London W1T 3QT

1 2 3 4 5 6 7 8 9 0

Contents

CHAPTER 1

The Science of the Mind

Demonstration

1.1   The Articulatory Rehearsal Loop

Cognitive psychology relies on a wide range of methods, many of which depend on precise measurement or subtle analyses of complex data patterns. However, many of the phenomena we observe in the lab can be demonstrated informally—either by you, the reader, working on your own, or in a classroom setting. In this workbook, therefore, I've provided a series of demonstrations illustrating some of the phenomena discussed in the text. I hope these demonstrations will help you sharpen your understanding of the data patterns; I hope the demonstrations will also make the data more concrete and more familiar, and hence more memorable.

As our initial example, Chapter 1 introduces the notion of the articulatory rehearsal loop, one of the key "helpers" within the working-memory system. As the chapter describes, many lines of evidence document the existence of this loop, but one type of evidence is especially easy to demonstrate.

Read these numbers and think about them for just a second, so that you'll be able to recall them in a few seconds: 8 2 5 7. Now, read the following paragraph:

You should, right now, be rehearsing those numbers while you are reading this paragraph, so that you'll be able to recall them when you're done with the paragraph. You are probably storing the numbers in your articulatory rehearsal loop, saying the numbers over and over to yourself. Using the loop in this way requires little effort or attention, and this leaves the central executive free to work on the concurrent task of reading these sentences—identifying the words, assembling them into phrases, and figuring out what the phrases mean. As a result, with the loop holding the numbers and the executive doing the reading, there is no conflict and no problem. Therefore, this combination is relatively easy.

Now, what were those numbers? Most people can recall them with no problem, for the reasons just described. They read—and understood—the passage, and holding on to the numbers caused no difficulty at all. Did *you* understand the passage? Can you summarize it, briefly, in your own words?

Next, try a variation: Again, you will place four numbers in memory, but then you will immediately start saying "Tah-Tah-Tah" over and over out loud, while reading a passage. Ready? The numbers are: 3 8 1 4. Start saying "Tah-Tah-Tah" and read on.

> Again, you should be rehearsing the numbers as you read, and also repeating "Tah-Tah-Tah" over and over out loud. The repetitions of "Tah-Tah-Tah" demand little thought, but they do require the neural circuits and the muscles that are needed for speaking, and with these resources tied up in this fashion, they're not available for use in the rehearsal loop. As a result, you don't have the option of storing the four numbers in the loop. That means you need to find some other means of remembering the numbers, and that is likely to involve the central executive. As a result, the executive needs to do two things at once—hold on to the numbers, and read the passage.

Now, what were those numbers? Many people in this situation find they have forgotten the numbers. Others can recall the numbers but find this version of the task (in which the executive couldn't rely on the rehearsal loop) much harder, and they may report that they actually found themselves skimming the passage, not reading it. Again, can you summarize the paragraph you just read? Glance back over the paragraph to see if your summary is complete; did you miss something? You may have, because many people report that in this situation their attention hops back and forth, so that they read a little, think about the numbers, read some more, think about the numbers again, and so on—an experience they didn't have without the "Tah-Tah-Tah."

Demonstration adapted from: Baddeley, A. (1986). *Working memory.* Oxford, England: Clarendon Press.

Applying Cognitive Psychology

Research Methods: Testable Hypotheses

Research in cognitive psychology can yield results that are both important and useful. These results have value, however, only if they are based on sound methods and good science. If not, we may be offering practical suggestions that do more harm than good, and we may be making theoretical claims that lead us away from the truth, not toward it.

For students learning about cognitive psychology, therefore, it is important to understand the methods that make our science possible. This will allow you to see why our results must be taken seriously and why we can, with confidence, draw the conclusions that we do. For this reason, I have written a brief Research Methods essay, highlighting a methodological issue or focusing on a research example, for each of the chapters in the text. I hope these essays will broaden your understanding of our methods and deepen your appreciation for why our results can be (indeed, *must be*) taken seriously. More broadly, these essays will help you understand more fully how our science proceeds.

First, though, we might ask: What *is* science, and what is it about cognitive psychology that makes it count as a science? The key lies in the idea that science cannot be based just on someone's opinions about the world or on someone's (perhaps biased) interpretation of the facts. Instead, a science needs to be based on the facts themselves, and that means the scientific community needs to check every one of its claims against the facts, to find out with certainty whether each claim is correct. If we learn that the evidence for a claim is weak or ambiguous, then we need to seek more evidence in order to achieve certainty. And, of course, if we learn that a claim does *not* fit with the facts, then we are obligated to set it aside, to make sure we only offer claims that we know are correct.

Clearly, then, the notion of *testing* our claims, to make sure they match the facts, is central for any science, and this has a powerful implication for how we formulate our claims in the first place. Specifically, we need to make sure that all of our claims are formulated in a way that will allow the testing that is central to the scientific enterprise; said differently, science is possible only if the claims being considered are rigorously *testable*. But how do we ensure testability? Among other points, we need to make certain our claims never rely on ambiguous terms or vague phrasing; we also need to avoid escape clauses like "Maybe this will happen" or "Sometimes we'll observe *X* and sometimes we won't."

To see how this plays out, consider the claim "No matter what day of the year you pick, someone famous was born on that day." Is this claim testable? Actually, it isn't. Imagine that the most prominent person you can think of, born on December 19, is Daniel Reisberg. Does this support the claim, because Reisberg is famous? (After all, thousands of students have read his books.) Or does it contradict the claim, because Reisberg isn't famous? (After all, most people have never heard of him.) Both of these positions seem sensible, and so our "test" of this claim about birthdays turns out to depend on opinion, not fact. If you hold the opinion that Reisberg is famous, then the evidence about the December 19 birthday confirms our claim; if you hold the opposite opinion, the same evidence *doesn't* confirm the claim. As a result, this claim is not testable—there's no way to say with certainty whether it fits with the facts or not.

Of course, we could make this claim testable if we could find a suitable definition of "famous." In that case, we could, with some certainty, decide whether Reisberg is famous or not, and then we could use this point to test our claim about birthdays. But until that is done, there is no way to test this claim in the fashion, not dependent on opinion, that science requires.

This example illustrates why a scientific hypothesis must be framed precisely—so that we can check the facts and then say with certainty whether the hypothesis is correct. But how do we check the facts? We'll explore this in upcoming Research Methods essays in this workbook.

FOR DISCUSSION

We often recite so-called words of wisdom to remind each other of how events in the world work: "Good things come in threes." "Absence makes the heart grow fonder." "Opposites attract." Choose one of these common expressions (perhaps one of the ones just mentioned, or some other). Does this expression offer a testable claim? If not, why not? How could you rephrase or elaborate on the expression (or, perhaps, define the terms used in the expression) to turn it into a testable claim?

Cognitive Psychology and Education: Enhancing Classroom Learning

There has long been a specialty known as *educational psychology*—a specialty that asks, in a scientific way, a variety of questions about how students learn, how they use what they learn, and what teachers can do to improve the educational process. Some of the questions within educational psychology are linked to issues of motivation: What is the best way to motivate students? Is praise effective? Should teachers give students certain performance goals? Growth goals? Should teachers reward students in some concrete way for reaching these goals?

Other questions in educational psychology are rooted in *developmental psychology*, as we try to figure out how the educational process needs to be tuned to match the developmental status of a growing child. Still other issues are tied to the broader field of *social psychology*: how students interact with each other and help each other; how teachers can encourage cooperation and good morale in the classroom; and so on.

But, of course, many questions in educational psychology are directly tied to issues within *cognitive psychology*: How can students more effectively get material into memory? How can students better retain what they've learned? How can students become better at solving problems or drawing conclusions? Questions like these are directly tied to the fundamental issues in play in all of the chapters in the textbook; therefore, I've written a brief Cognitive Psychology and Education essay for each chapter, applying the claims and methods developed in that chapter to some important aspect of classroom learning.

Certain educational issues are covered directly in the text itself. Chapter 5, for example, talks about how material is entered into memory, and the studies described in the chapter have obvious and immediate implications for your classroom work. Likewise, Chapter 14 talks about different strategies you can use, during learning, to increase the chances that you will be able to draw analogies from what you have learned, helping you to solve problems you encounter in the future. But in other cases the educational implications will be less obvious, and so these essays will provide a venue through which to explore those implications more closely.

I've framed these essays so that they will be immediately useful for students reading this workbook as part of a college or university course. In short, I want to see if I can use the lessons of cognitive psychology to help you become a better student. I've also framed most of these essays as responses to questions that I've gotten many times from my own students. Like all students, they want to maximize their performance, and they realize that my courses deal with issues that are directly relevant to their daily activities—their *reading* (and so they ask me about speed-reading), *learning* (and so they ask me how to study), *taking tests* (and so they ask me about test strategies), and more. I address their questions in these essays, and in the process I hope to teach you more about cognitive psychology and also provide you with information you can immediately use.

Cognitive Psychology and the Law: Improving the Criminal Justice System

Research in cognitive psychology can help us understand deep theoretical issues, such as what it means to be rational or what the function of consciousness might be. But our research also has pragmatic implications, with our studies often providing important lessons for how we should conduct our day-to-day lives. Some of those pragmatic lessons are obvious. For example, students can use knowledge about learning and memory to choose effective study strategies. Some implications of our work, though, are less obvious—for example, the implications of cognitive psychology for the criminal justice system.

How is our science relevant to police work or the courts? To answer this question, think about what happens in a criminal investigation. Eyewitnesses provide evidence, based on what they paid attention to during a crime and what they remember. Police officers question the witnesses, trying to maximize what each witness recalls—but without leading the witness in any way. Then the police try to deduce, from the evidence, who the perpetrator was. Then later, during the trial, jurors must listen to evidence and make a judgment about the defendant's innocence or guilt.

Cast in these terms, it should be obvious that an understanding of *attention*, *memory*, *reasoning*, and *judgment* (to name just a few processes) are directly relevant to what happens in the legal system. Indeed, we can plausibly hope to use what we know about these processes to improve the courts' procedures—for example, to design more effective ways to question witnesses (*memory*), to help jurors do their job (*judgment*), and so on.

Drawing on these points, I provide a supplemental Cognitive Psychology and the Law essay for every chapter of the textbook, describing how the materials in that chapter can help you to understand a specific aspect of the criminal justice system. These essays will illustrate how cognitive psychology can be brought to bear on issues of enormous importance, issues that are in obvious ways rather distant from the laboratory.

Let's add, though, that other essays could highlight cognitive psychology's contributions to other real-world concerns. Why, therefore, should we focus on the criminal justice system? There are several reasons, but one prominent motivation is my own involvement with these issues: As a psychologist specializing in memory, I often consult with police, lawyers, and the courts on questions about eyewitness evidence. This work allows me, as a scientist, to play a small part in improving the criminal justice system in my corner of the United States—a point that gives me enormous satisfaction, speaking both as an academic and as a citizen.

My work with the courts provides a frequent reminder for me that our science does indeed generate knowledge that really is important, useful, and sometimes surprising. At the same time, though, my work with the courts sometimes reminds me of the *limitations* of our science, and that is also important. For example, when we study how someone pays attention to shapes on a computer screen, can we draw conclusions about how an eyewitness pays attention to a complex and rapidly unfolding crime? When we study how someone memorizes a list of words, does this tell us how a crime victim remembers a robbery? These are important questions, and the answers need to be thought through with care. For now, though, let's focus just on these questions themselves—and celebrate the fact that psychology's partnership with the criminal justice system forces us to take these questions very seriously—and that has to improve how, as scientists, we think about these issues.

CHAPTER 2

The Neural Basis for Cognition

Demonstrations

2.1   Foveation

The chapter describes the basic anatomy of the eyeball, including the fact that the *retina* (the light-sensitive surface at the back of the eyeball) has, at its center, a specialized region called the fovea. The cells in the fovea are much better at discerning visual detail than cells elsewhere on the retina. Therefore, if you want to scrutinize a scene, you need to move your eyes—so that first *this* bit of the visual world falls onto the fovea, and then *that* bit. Eye movements, however, are surprisingly slow (roughly five per second), and this places severe limits on your pickup of information from the world. These limits, in turn, influence how the nervous system can use and interpret the information actually received.

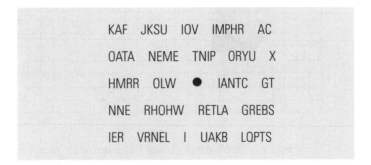

Just how distinctive is the fovea? Hold the book about 12 inches from your face. Point your eyes at the black dot in the middle of this display, and try not to move them. Stare at the dot for a moment, to make sure you've got your eye position appropriately "locked" in place, and then, without moving your eyes, try to read the letters one or two rows away from the dot, or a couple of positions to the left or right. You should be able to do this, but you will probably find that your impression of the letters is indistinct. Now—still without moving your eyes—try reading the letters further from the dot. This should be more difficult.

What's going on? When you point your eyes at the dot, you are positioning each eyeball relative to the page so that the dot falls on the fovea; therefore, the other letters fall on retinal positions away from the fovea. Acuity—the ability to see detail—falls off rapidly if the image is not on the fovea, and that is why some of the letters in the figure appeared quite blurry: They were falling on areas of the retina that are literally less able to see sharply.

Notice, though, that in the ordinary circumstances of day-to-day life the entire visual world seems sharp and clear to you. You don't have an impression of being able to see a small region clearly, with everything else being blurry. Part of the reason is that you (unconsciously) fill in a lot of detail, making inferences and extrapolations about things you cannot see.

2.2 The Blind Spot and the Active Nature of Vision

Axons from the retina's ganglion cells gather together to form the optic nerve. At the point where these axons exit the retina, there's no space left over for any other type of cell. Therefore, there can be no photoreceptors at that location, and so no way to detect light if it falls on that location. As a result, you are quite literally blind to any information falling onto that spot—hence, the name "blind spot." Ordinarily, people are not aware of the blind spot—but we can make them aware with a simple procedure.

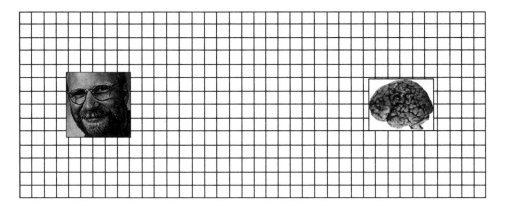

Hold the book about 18 inches from your face. Close your left eye. Stare at the center of the picture of the book's author on the left. Gradually move the book toward or away from your nose. At most distances, you'll still be able to see the brain (on the right) out of the corner of your eye. You should be able to find a distance, though, at which the brain drops from view—it just seems not to be there.

What is going on? You've positioned the book, relative to your eye, in a fashion that places the author's picture on your fovea but the picture of the brain on your *blind spot* and so the brain simply became invisible to you.

Notice, though, that even when the brain "disappeared," you did not perceive a "hole" in the visual world. In particular, the brain disappeared, but you could still perceive the continuous grid pattern with no interruption in the lines. Why is this? Your visual system detected the pattern in the grid (continuous vertical lines + continuous horizontals) and used this pattern to "fill in" the information that was missing because of the blind spot. But, of course, the picture of the brain is not part of this overall pattern, and so it was not included when you did the filling in. Therefore, the picture of the brain vanished, but the pattern was not disrupted.

2.3   A Brightness Illusion

The first two demonstrations for this chapter have emphasized the active nature of vision—in filling in what you can see outside of the fovea, or filling in the information missing from the visual input because of the blind spot. Vision's active role is also evident in many illusions—for example, in the faint gray "dots" you see where the white bars in this figure cross.

There are no dots at those intersections. The white bars are uniform in brightness from the far left to the far right, and from the top to the bottom. (If you don't believe this, cover the figure with two pieces of paper, adjusting them to expose a single white bar.) Why do you see the dots? They are the result of lateral inhibition: At positions *away from* those intersections (e.g., in the center of the white bars, midway between the intersections), each portion of the white bars is surrounded by more white on just two sides—to the left and right, or above and below. At the intersections, each bit of the white is surrounded by more white *on all four sides*—to the left and right, *and* above and below. Each of these neighboring regions produces lateral inhibition, and so the white regions at the intersections are receiving, in effect, twice as much inhibition as the white regions away from the intersections.

Because of this inhibition, the white regions at the intersections literally send a weaker signal to the brain—and so are perceived as less bright. The visual system is receiving the same *input* from the white regions at the intersections (because the brightness, at these regions, is objectively the same as the brightness elsewhere on the white bars). However, the visual system responds differently to this input depending on where in the pattern it is—thanks to the lateral inhibition. This produces the sense of the faint gray dots at the intersections—an instance in which the setup of the visual system is clearly shaping (and, in this case, distorting) what you see.

Applying Cognitive Psychology

Research Methods: Control Groups

In Chapter 2, we talk several times about this or that brain area being activated during some particular activity—so that certain areas in the occipital lobe (for example) are especially active when someone is examining a visual stimulus, certain areas of the frontal lobe are especially active when someone is listening to a verbal input, and so on. We need to be clear, though, about what these claims really mean.

All cells in the brain are active all the time. When they receive some input, however, or when they are working on a particular process, the brain cells change their activation level. Therefore, when we talk about, say, the occipital lobe's response to a visual input, we do not mean that the cells are active when an input arrives and inactive the rest of the time. Instead, we're saying that when a visual input arrives, the activity in the occipital lobe increases from its prior (*baseline*) level.

To measure these increases, though, we need a basis for comparison. Indeed, this is a feature of virtually all scientific investigation: We often can interpret a fact, a measurement, or an observation only with reference to some appropriate baseline. This is true outside of science as well. Imagine that your school's football team wins 90% of its games when you're wearing your lucky socks. Does this mean the socks are helpful? We'd need to ask how often the team wins when you're *not* wearing your lucky socks; if that number is also 90%, then your socks have no effect at all. If the number is 95%, then your socks might actually be a jinx!

In scientific research, our basis for comparison, in evaluating our data, is provided by a *control condition*—a condition that allows us to see how things unfold in the absence of the experimental manipulation. If, therefore, we want to understand how the brain responds to visual inputs, we need to compare a condition with a visual input (the *experimental condition*) with a control condition lacking this input. The difference between the conditions is usually created by the *independent variable*—a single factor that differentiates the two conditions. The independent variable might be the presence or absence of your lucky socks in our football example, or the presence or absence of a visual input in our brain example. (In both cases we have *one* variable, and *two possible values* that the variable can take, within our experiment.)

The independent variable is sometimes instead called the *predictor variable*, because our comparison is asking whether we can use this variable to predict the experiment's outcome. (Does the presence of your lucky socks predict a greater chance of winning? Is the presence of a visual input associated with greater brain activity, so that when the input is on the scene we can predict that the activity will increase?)

Not surprisingly, the variable we measure in our data collection is called the *dependent variable*, so that our study is asking, in essence, whether this variable depends on the predictor variable. In many cases, the dependent variable is straightforward (What was the score of the game? What is the level of brain activity?), but sometimes it is not. We will return to this topic in the Research Methods essay for Chapter 14.

We still need to ask, however, exactly how we should set up our study, and how in particular we should set up the control condition. Imagine, as one possibility, that participants in our experimental condition are staring attentively at a computer screen, eagerly awaiting (and eventually seeing) a visual stimulus, while the participants in our control condition are told merely to hang out, so that we can observe the functioning of their brains. If we found differences between these two conditions, we could draw no conclusions. That's because any differences we observe might be due to the presence of the visual stimulus in one condition and not the other, or they might be due to the fact that participants in one condition are attentive while those in the other condition are relaxed. With no way to choose between these options, we'd have no way to interpret the data.

Clearly, then, our control condition must be carefully designed so that it differs from the experimental condition in just one way (in our example, in the presence or absence of the visual stimulus). With this, we want to make sure that participants in the two conditions get similar instructions and have similar expectations for the experiment. Only then will the contrast between the conditions be meaningful, allowing us to interpret the data and thus to properly test our hypothesis.

FOR DISCUSSION

We know that people often experience *auditory imagery*—hearing a sound (a favorite song, perhaps) playing "in their heads," even though no actual sound is present in their environment. Subjectively, auditory images seem to resemble actual hearing—you experience the image as having a certain tempo, a certain sequence of pitches, and so on. But what is the biological basis for auditory imagery?

Imagine that you wanted to test this hypothesis: "Auditory imagery relies on brain areas similar to those used by actual hearing." What conditions would you want to study in order to test this hypothesis? First, you would need to think about what instructions you could give your research participants to make sure they were engaging in auditory imagery during the time in which you monitored their brain activity. Second, you would need to choose what task you'd give to research participants in the control condition. Actually, you might consider having *two* control conditions—one that involves actual *hearing* with an overt stimulus, and one that involves neither actual hearing nor auditory imagery. That way, you could show that the brain activity during imagery was *similar to* that of the "hearing" control group, but *different from* that of the "not hearing" group. What might your other two control groups involve—what tasks would participants in these groups do, or what instructions would you give them, while you were monitoring their brain activity?

Cognitive Psychology and Education:
Using Biology to Improve Memory

Advertisers offer a range of food supplements that supposedly will make you smarter, improve your memory, help you think more clearly, and so on. Unfortunately, though, these food supplements have usually not been tested in any systematic way. (In the United States and in many other countries, new medicines are tested before they are put on the market, but new food supplements are not.) In most cases, therefore, the claims made about these food supplements are simply unsupported by evidence. Worse, in at least some cases, the food supplements have turned out to have harmful side effects, making the lack of testing rather alarming.

One supplement, though, has been widely endorsed and rigorously tested; this supplement is *Ginkgo biloba*, an extract derived from a tree of the same name and advertised as capable of enhancing memory.

In evaluating the effects of *Ginkgo biloba*, it is important to bear in mind that memory depends on the brain, and brain functioning is, from the body's point of view, enormously expensive: To do its normal work, the brain requires an excellent blood flow and, with that, a lot of oxygen and a lot of nutrients. Indeed, it is sometimes estimated that the brain, constituting just 2% of our body weight, consumes 15% percent of our body's energy supply!

It's not surprising, therefore, that the brain is influenced by almost any change in your health. If you are tired, not eating enough, or ill, these conditions will affect all of your bodily functions; but since the brain needs so much energy, these health concerns often cause problems in brain functioning that appear sooner than problems elsewhere in the body. Conversely, a healthy diet, adequate exercise, and regular sleeping hours will improve the performance of all your bodily systems; but again, since the brain is so expensive to maintain, these different aspects of a healthy lifestyle will all help you to think more clearly, pay attention more closely, and learn more effectively. The implications of this for students are clear.

But what about *Ginkgo biloba*? Evidence suggests that *Ginkgo* extract may improve blood circulation, reduce some sorts of bodily inflammation, and protect the nervous system from several types of damage. This is why researchers are examining this extract as a possible treatment for people who have troubles with blood circulation or who are at risk for nerve damage. In fact, results suggest that patients with Huntingdon's disease, Alzheimer's disease, and several other conditions may be helped by this food supplement. Let's be clear, though, that the *Ginkgo* is not directly making these patients "smarter." Instead, it is broadly improving their blood circulation and the health status of their nerve cells, allowing these cells to do their work.

What about healthy people—people not suffering from various bodily inflammations or damage to their brain cells? Here the evidence is mixed. Some reviews have offered the tentative conclusion that *Ginkgo* may improve the cognitive functioning of healthy young adults, but many studies have failed to observe any benefit from this food supplement, suggesting that *Ginkgo*'s effects, if they exist at all in healthy adults, are so small that they are difficult to detect.

Are there other steps or other food supplements that are more promising and that *will* improve the mental functioning of healthy young adults? We have already indicated part of a positive answer: Overall, good nutrition, plenty of sleep, adequate exercise, and so on will keep you healthy and keep your blood supply in good condition, and this will help your brain to do its job. In addition, there may be something else you can do: The brain's functioning depends on an adequate fuel supply, and that fuel supply comes from the sugar *glucose*. When you are doing mental work (e.g., when you're paying close attention to a lecture, or trying to solve a problem), this mental activity is supported by brain areas that require glucose, and if there's not enough glucose available, brain functioning will be diminished.

You can actually protect yourself, therefore, by making sure that your brain has all the glucose it needs. This is *not* a recommendation to jettison all other aspects of your diet and eat nothing but chocolate bars. However, a cup of sweetened tea, a glass of lemonade, or a small candy bar may help you just before you take an exam or as you sit in a particularly challenging class. These steps will help ensure that you're not caught by a glucose shortfall that could interfere with your brain's functioning.

Let's be cautious, though, in how we think about these points. As one concern, you don't want to gulp down *too much* sugar; if you do, you might produce an upward spike in your blood sugar followed by a sudden drop, and this can produce problems of its own. In addition, we should emphasize that the benefits of sugar—even if you get the "dose" right—may be relatively small. This is because the glucose supply for the brain is tightly controlled by a number of different mechanisms inside the body, and these mechanisms usually guarantee that your brain gets all the sugar it needs. As a result, the extra sugar from a candy bar or glass of lemonade may just get "set aside" by the liver, and not be sent to the brain at all.

To put this point a different way, the benefits are likely to be much larger from other steps we've mentioned, and from other steps you already know about, based on common sense: It really does help, for example, to keep yourself healthy and well rested, and to try your best to pay attention. These simple, broad measures are usually effective, and they stand in contrast to the small benefit you might obtain from gobbling a chocolate bar just before your Bio exam.

In short, then, the evidence suggests that there is no "fast track" toward better cognition; no pill or sugary drink will dramatically improve your mental performance. The best path toward better cognition seems, in some ways, to be the one that common sense would already recommend.

For more on this topic

Gold, P. E., Cahill, L., & Wenk, G. L. (2002). *Ginkgo biloba*: A cognitive enhancer? *Psychological Science in the Public Interest, 3*, 2–11.

Masicampo, E., & Baumeister, R. (2008). Toward a physiology of dual-process reasoning and judgment: Lemonade, willpower, and expensive rule-based analysis. *Psychological Science, 19*, 255–260.

McDaniel, M. A., Maier, S. F., & Einstein, G. O. (2002). "Brain-specific" nutrients: A memory cure? *Psychological Science in the Public Interest, 3*, 12–38.

Cognitive Psychology and the Law: Detecting Lies

It is obvious that people sometimes lie to the police, and, of course, the police do all they can to detect this deception. Some police officers claim that they can tell, during an interview, whether a suspect is lying to them or not; but, in truth, most people (and most police) are not very skilled in making this determination. This is one of the reasons why law enforcement often relies on a machine called the *polygraph*, or, as it's more commonly known, the lie detector. This device is designed to measure moment-by-moment changes in someone's breathing, heart rate, blood pressure, or amount of perspiration. To use these measurements for lie detection, we rely on the fact that someone who is lying is likely to become anxious about the lie, or tense. These emotional changes, even if carefully hidden by the test subject, are associated with changes in the biological markers measured by the polygraph; thus, by using the polygraph to detect these changes, we detect the lie.

Unfortunately, though, this procedure is of questionable value. The polygraph often fails to detect lies, and—just as bad—the test often indicates that people are lying when they are not. The reason is simple: Sometimes liars are perfectly calm and not at all tense, and the polygraph will therefore miss their lies; sometimes truth-tellers are highly anxious, and the polygraph will pick this up. In addition, it is possible to "beat the test" by using certain strategies. One strategy is for the test subject to engage in fast-paced mental arithmetic during key parts of the test. (Most polygraph tests compare the subject's state when he's just been asked crucial questions—such as "Did you rob the bank?"—in comparison to his state when he's just been asked neutral questions—such as "What is your name?" If the test subject uses a strategy that increases his arousal during the *neutral* questions, this will make it harder to detect any difference between his state during these questions and during the crucial questions, making it harder to detect lies!)

A different lie-detection technique is less commonly used, but more promising. The *Guilty Knowledge Test* (GKT) doesn't rely on measurements of stress or tension in order to detect the lie. Instead, the test seeks to detect the *cognition* associated with lying. Specifically, the test relies on the fact that in many crimes there will be certain details that no one knows other than the police and the guilty party. This allows the police to ask questions like, "Was the injured woman's scarf: (a) red? (b) green? (c) blue? (d) white?" A criminal might refuse to answer, claiming to have no knowledge; but even so, the criminal will almost certainly show an *orienting response* when the correct answer is mentioned. It is as if the criminal cannot help "perking up" in response to the one option that's familiar and cannot help thinking, "Yes, that was it," even though he overtly insists that he does not know the answer.

The orienting response involves changes in the electrical activity of the brain, and these changes can be detected by suitable measurements on the surface of the scalp. In this way, the orienting response can be objectively recorded even if the criminal denies any knowledge of the crime.

The orienting response itself is relatively easy to detect, and studies show that a reliance on this detection does allow the GKT to do a good job of detecting "guilty knowledge"—knowledge that only a crime's perpetrator would know, which in turn allows the GKT to identify the perpetrator. However, the GKT has limits. The test can be run only if the police can identify an adequate number of test items (i.e., facts that the perpetrator would certainly know but that no one else would); the accuracy of the GKT falls if the number of test items is too small. Even with these limits, though, the GKT is being adopted by some law enforcement agencies.

It appears, then, that our understanding of the brain, and how people react to meaningful stimuli, can provide an important new tool for the detection of guilty knowledge, and thus the detection of lies.

For more on this topic

Ben-Shakhar, G., Bar-Hillel, M., & Kremnitzer, M. (2002). Trial by polygraph: Reconsidering the use of the Guilty Knowledge Technique in court. *Law and Human Behavior, 26,* 527–541.

Honts, C., et al. (1994). Mental and physical countermeasures reduce the accuracy of polygraph tests. *Journal of Applied Psychology, 79,* 252–259.

FOR DISCUSSION

Imagine that you are in charge of law enforcement for your city or for your state or province. Given the information you just read, what policy or procedural changes would you want to consider—things you should start doing or things you should stop doing? Or would you delay taking action until more data were available on this topic? What sorts of data?

You might also give some thought to the fact that most tests of the GKT are done *in the laboratory:* Volunteers in these studies are encouraged to lie about certain points, and then the researchers try to detect these lies by using the GKT. But, of course, volunteers in a lab might be different from perpetrators of actual crimes; thus, the GKT might detect (relatively minor) lies in the lab, but it might not detect (much more consequential) lies involving a real crime. What sort of steps might you take to make the lab studies as realistic as possible, in order to maximize the chances that the lab data could be generalized to real-world settings? What sorts of studies might you design "in the field"—perhaps with suspects in real criminal cases—that might tell you if the GKT works as proposed in actual criminal investigations?

CHAPTER 3

Recognizing Objects

Demonstrations

3.1   Adelson's Brightness Illusion

There was a common theme in Chapter 2's demonstrations: The visual system does not just "receive" visual input the way that, say, a camera might. Instead, the visual system actively shapes the input—altering some bits, emphasizing other bits, adding information where needed. This active nature is evident in many ways—including cases in which the visual system *distorts* the input in a fashion that leads to an illusion.

   Examine this figure (designed by Edward Adelson) carefully. Look at the color of the "middle square" (third row, third column) and also the color of the square marked with the arrow. See how different they are? Actually, the two are the exact same shade on the page. If you don't believe this, try blocking out the rest of the figure—with pieces of paper, perhaps, or your fingers—so that all you can see is these two squares. When they are isolated in this way, it becomes clear that they are, in fact, the exact same brightness.

What produces this illusion? Two factors contribute. First, the "middle" square is surrounded by dark squares, and these, by contrast, make it look brighter. The square marked with the arrow, on the other hand, is surrounded by brighter regions, and these, by contrast, make it look darker. This contrast effect depends on mechanisms similar to the ones that produced the illusion in Demonstration 3 for Chapter 2 in this workbook; the mechanisms are closely linked to what we described in the textbook's Chapter 2 when we talked about lateral inhibition.

This demonstration, however, also introduces a new factor, and it's part of the reason why this illusion is so compelling. In this figure, you are influenced by the shadow cast by the cylinder. In the figure, the shadow appears to fall over the middle square, so that (presumably) it is receiving less illumination than the square marked with the arrow. Unconsciously, you take this difference in illumination into account: In essence, you say to yourself, "If it appears in this way with so little light shining on it, then what would it look like if it were brightly lit?" This leads you to adjust your perception of its brightness, causing it to seem brighter than it actually is.

The illusion here is powerful, and so it serves as a powerful reminder of how much *interpretive work* we do with visual input.

Demonstration adapted from: Adelson, E. (2000). Lightness perception and lightness illusions. In M. Gazzaniga (Ed.), *The new cognitive neurosciences* (2nd ed., pp. 339–351). Cambridge, MA: MIT Press.

3.2   Features and Feature Combinations

The chapter discusses the importance of *features* in our recognition of objects, and it argues that features are detected by a separate level of detectors, early in the sequence of events that eventually leads to the recognition of such things as chairs and dogs and trees and houses. This priority of features is, in fact, easy to demonstrate.

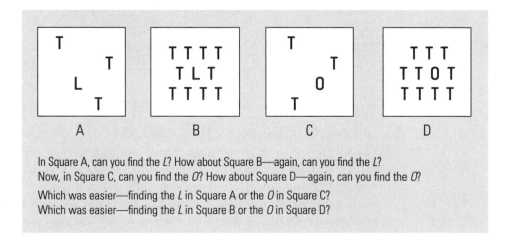

In Square A, can you find the *L*? How about Square B—again, can you find the *L*?
Now, in Square C, can you find the *O*? How about Square D—again, can you find the *O*?

Which was easier—finding the *L* in Square A or the *O* in Square C?
Which was easier—finding the *L* in Square B or the *O* in Square D?

Most people find the search in Square A (finding the *L*) harder and slower than the search in Square C (finding the *O*). This makes sense: The *L*- and *T*-shapes in Square A have the same features; they differ only in how the features are joined together. Therefore, finding the target requires you to think about how the features are put together. In contrast, the *O*- and *T*-shapes in Square C have very different features, and so now finding the target requires you only to identify these features, with no attention to how the features are assembled. In general, searches for a feature are much easier than searches for a feature combination, highlighting the importance of features as a basis for our perception.

How big a difference was there between searching for the *L* when it was hidden among three *T*'s (Square A) and when it was hidden among ten *T*'s (Square B)? How big a difference was there with the *O*, comparing the search in Square C with the search in Square D?

Most people find little difference between Square C and Square D: In both cases, the target (the *O*) just pops out at you, and it doesn't much matter whether you're searching for the *O* among four items (Square C) or eleven (Square D). In contrast, there *is* a difference between Squares A and B—with Square B being harder for most people. When you're searching for a *combination* for features, there's no "pop out." Instead, you need to examine the forms one by one, and so Square B (with eleven shapes to examine) takes more time than Square A.

Demonstration adapted from: Thornton, T., & Gilden, D. (2007). Parallel and serial processes in visual search. *Psychological Review, 114,* 71–103.

3.3   Inferences in Reading

The role of *inferences* within the normal process of reading is easy to demonstrate. Remarkably, you make these inferences even when you don't want to—that is, even when you're trying to read carefully. To see this, count how many times the letter *F* appears in the following passage:

FINISHED FILES ARE THE RESULT

OF YEARS OF SCIENTIFIC STUDY

COMBINED WITH THE EXPERIENCE

OF YEARS.

The correct answer is *six*; did you find them all?

Many people miss one or two or even three of the *F*s. Why is this?

In normal reading, we do not look at every letter, identifying it before we move on to the next. If we did, reading would be impossibly slow. (We can only move our eyes four or five times each second. If we looked at every letter, we'd only be able to read about five characters per second, or three hundred characters per minute. For most material, we actually read at a rate four or five times faster than this.)

How, then, do we read? We let our eyes hop along each line of print, relying on inference to fill in the information that our eyes are skipping over. As the text chapter describes, this process is made possible by the "inferential" character of our recognition network, and is enormously efficient. However, the process also risks error—because our inferences sometimes are wrong, and because we can sometimes miss something (a specific word or letter) that we are hunting for—as in this demonstration.

The process of skipping and making inferences is especially likely when the words in the text are *predictable*. If (for example) a sentence uses the phrase "the first word, the second, and the third," you surely know what the eighth word in this sequence ("third") will be without looking at it carefully. As a result, this is a word you're particularly likely to skip over as you read along. By the same logic, the word "of" is often quite predictable in many sentences, and so you probably missed one of the three *F*s appearing in the word "of." (The *f* in "of" is also hard to spot for another reason: Many people search for the *f* by *sounding out* the sentence and listening for the [f] sound. Of course, "of" is pronounced as though it ended with a *v*, not an *f*, and so it doesn't contain the sound people are hunting for.)

Note in addition that this process of skipping and inferring is so well practiced and so routine that we cannot "turn off" the process, even when we want to. This is why proofreading is usually difficult, as we skip by (and so overlook) our own errors. It is also why this demonstration works—because we have a hard time forcing ourselves into a letter-by-letter examination of the text, even when we want to.

Applying Cognitive Psychology

Research Methods: Dealing With Confounds

Imagine an experiment in which research participants are asked to recognize letter strings briefly presented on a computer screen—let's say for 30 milliseconds, followed by a mask. In the first 50 trials, the letter strings are random sequences ("okbo," "pmla," and so on). In the next 50 trials, the letter strings are all common four-letter words ("book," "lamp," "tree," and so on). Let's say that the participants are able, on average, to identify 30% of the random sequences and 65% of the words. This is a large difference; what should we conclude from it?

In fact, we can conclude nothing from this (fictional) experiment, because the procedure just described is flawed. The data tell us that participants did much better with the words, but why is this? One possibility is that words are, in fact, easier to recognize than nonwords. A different possibility, however, is that we are instead seeing an effect of *practice*: Maybe the participants did better with the word trials not because words are special, but simply because the words came later in the experiment, after the participants had gained some experience with the procedure. Likewise, participants did worse with the nonwords not because these are hard to recognize, but because they were presented before any practice or warm-up.

To put this in technical terms, the experiment just described is *invalid*—that is, it does not measure what it is intended to measure, namely, the difference between words and nonwords. The experiment is invalid because a *confound* is present—an extra variable that could have caused the observed data pattern. The confound is the *sequence*, and the confound makes the data ambiguous: Maybe words were better recognized because they're words, *or* maybe the words were better recognized simply because they came second. With no way in these data to choose between these interpretations, we cannot say which is the correct interpretation, and hence we can draw no conclusions from the experiment.

How should this experiment have been designed? One possibility is to *counterbalance* the sequence of trials: For half of the participants, we would show the words first, then the random letters; for the other half, we would use the reverse order. This setup doesn't eliminate the effect of practice, but it ensures that practice has the same impact on both conditions, and that's why we say the effect of practice is counterbalanced. Specifically, practice would help the words half the time (for the participants who got nonwords first), and it would help the nonwords half the time (for participants who got words first). If, therefore, we observe a difference between the conditions, it cannot be a result of practice: Practice should, in this situation, have the exact same effect on both conditions, and so it could not possibly cause a *difference* between the conditions.

As it turns out, we know how this experiment would turn out when properly done—words are, in fact, easier to recognize. Our point here, though, lies in what it takes for the experiment to be "properly done." In this and in all experiments, we need to remove confounds so that we can be sure what lies beneath the data pattern. There are various techniques available for dealing with confounds; we've mentioned just one of them (counterbalancing) here. The key, though, is that the confounds must be removed; only then can we legitimately draw conclusions from the experiment.

FOR DISCUSSION

Imagine that your friend Peter is convinced that it's easier to read print written on *yellow* paper than it is to read print written on ordinary *white* paper. You think this is wrong, but you decide to put Peter's hypothesis to the test. You therefore print a newspaper editorial on white paper and a news article on yellow paper. You recruit ten friends, and first you have them read the editorial (on white paper), and then you test their comprehension of it. Next, you have them read the news article (on yellow paper), and you test their comprehension of it. You find that they have better comprehension for the news article, and so you conclude (to your surprise!) that Peter is correct.

Is this conclusion justified? Or are there confounds here that make it impossible to draw any conclusions from this experiment? If there are confounds, how could you counterbalance the experiment so that the confounds are no longer a problem? (Be careful here, because there are *two* confounds in the experiment just described; how could you arrange the counterbalancing to make sure that *both* confounds are removed?)

Notice that the particular confounds you encounter can vary from one experiment to the next. However, some confounds come up over and over, and so it's good to be alert to them. One of these is *sequence*—which test comes first, and which comes later. Another common confound is *stimulus differences* —so that one condition involves easier materials, and one involves harder materials. A third

common confound is the *participants' expectations*—so that they might come into one condition with a certain set of biases or a certain motivation, and they might come into another condition with a different perspective. A fourth is *gender*, or *intelligence level*, or *any other background factor* that shapes who the participants are; these factors should be matched in the experimental and control groups. Yet another is *manner of recruitment*—so that it is problematic if one group of participants is filled with volunteers, and the other group is filled with people who are forced to be in the experiment (e.g., as a course requirement). This could easily shape the attitudes and motivations that the participants bring to the study. Can you think of other common confounds?

Cognitive Psychology and Education: Speed-Reading

Students usually have many pages of reading to do each week, and so they often wish they could read more quickly. Can we help them? Can we, in particular, help people to speed-read? In fact, it's easy to teach people to speed-read, and with just a little practice you can increase your reading speed by 50% or more. However, it is important to understand why speed-reading works, because this will help you see when speed-reading is a good idea—and when it is a disaster!

The text chapter emphasized that people don't look at each letter when they are reading. Instead, they look at some of the letters and use a sophisticated inference process to fill in what they've skipped. This process works roughly the same way in reading larger portions of text: You can skip many of the words and rely on inferences to plug the gaps. This is because the text that you read is often redundant, with many of the words being predictable from the context. You can save time, therefore, by skipping along and relying on rapid inference to cover the skips.

To develop this process into speed-reading, what you need to do is increase the skips and, with that, increase the use of inference. As a result, speed-reading is not really "reading faster," it is instead "reading *less* and inferring more." How does this work, and how can we make sure you will still end up understanding the material you've "read"?

First, before you try to speed-read some text, you need to lay the groundwork for the inference process—so that you'll make the inferences efficiently and accurately. Specifically, before you try to speed-read a text, you should flip through it quickly. Look at the figures and the figure captions. If there's a summary at the end or a preview at the beginning, read that. If there are headings and subheadings scattered through the text, read those. Each of these steps will give you a broad sense of what the material you're about to speed-read is all about, and that broad sense will prepare you to make rapid—and accurate—inferences about the material.

Second, make sure you do rely on inference; otherwise, you'll slide back into your habits of looking too carefully at the page and not relying enough on inference. To achieve this, read for a while holding an index card just under the line you are reading, or perhaps using your finger to slide along the lines of print, marking what you are reading at that moment. These procedures establish a physical marker of where you are on the page, a "pointer" that keeps track of where you are as you move from word to word. This use of a pointer will become easy and automatic after a few minutes of practice, and once it does, you're ready for the next step.

Now try moving the index card, or sliding your finger along, just a bit faster than feels comfortable, and try to move your eyes to keep up with this marker. This, too, will become easier with just a bit of practice. Don't try to go too fast; you'll know if you are moving too swiftly if you suddenly realize that you don't have a clue what's on the page. Move quickly enough so that you can grasp what's on the page, but so that you feel you have to hustle along to keep up with your pointer.

You may want to practice this for a couple of days, and as you do, you'll learn to move the pointer faster and faster. As a result, you'll learn to increase your reading speed by 30%, or 40%, or more. But let's be clear about what's going on here: You are not learning (as ads sometimes claim) to "see more in a single glance." (That wouldn't be possible unless we rewire your eyeballs, and that's not going to happen.) Instead, you are simply shifting the balance between how much input you're taking in and how much you're filling in the gaps with sophisticated guesswork.

On this basis, you can easily see that speed-reading is a good bet if you are reading redundant or repetitive material; that's a situation in which your inferences about the skipped words are likely to be correct, and so you might as well use the faster process of making inferences, rather than the slower process of looking at individual words. By the same logic, though, speed-reading is a bad bet if the material is hard to understand; in that case, you won't be able to figure out the skipped words via inference, and then speed-reading will hurt you. Speed-reading is also a bad bet if you're trying to appreciate an author's style. Imagine, for example, that you speed-read Shakespeare's *Romeo and Juliet*. You probably will be able to speed-read and make inferences about the plot. (After all, the plot is simple: Romeo and Juliet are in love. Their families oppose the romance. In the end, everyone dies.) But you probably won't be able to make inferences about the specific words you're skipping over, and thus inferences about the *language* that Shakespeare actually used (unless you happen to be just as good a writer as Shakespeare was). And, of course, if you miss the language of Shakespeare and miss the poetry, you've missed the point.

Do practice speed-reading, and do use it when text-guided inference will serve you well. This will allow you to zoom through many texts, and it will dramatically decrease the time you need for at least some of your reading. But do not speed-read material that is technical, filled with specific details that you'll need, or beautiful for its language. In those cases, what you want is to pay attention to the words on the page, and not rely on your own inferences.

Cognitive Psychology and the Law: Cross-Race Identification

In Chapter 3 of the textbook, we argue that people use two different mechanisms for recognizing the stimuli they encounter. One mechanism is *feature based*, and it works by first identifying the input's parts. These parts are then assembled into larger and larger wholes until the entire input is identified. The other recognition mechanism is *configuration based*. It is less concerned with individual features, but it is exquisitely sensitive to the overall arrangement in the input.

The second of these mechanisms, relying on configurations, is crucial when we are recognizing faces, but we also use it in other settings: Expert bird watchers, for example, seem to use this mechanism when making distinctions among different types of birds; expert dog-show judges rely on it to recognize individual dogs. Overall, it seems that people use the configuration-based mechanism whenever they are identifying individuals within an enormously familiar category.

How is this pertinent to law enforcement? Imagine that you witness a crime. From the information you provide, the police develop a hypothesis about who the perpetrator might have been. They place the suspect's photo on a page together with five other photos and show you this "photospread." Will you recognize the perpetrator within this group? If so, this provides important evidence confirming the police officers' suspicions.

In this situation, your ability to identify the perpetrator depends on many factors, including the suspect's *race*. This is because people are much better at recognizing individuals from their own race than they are in recognizing individuals from other races. Indeed, if the criminal is present in the photospread, witnesses are roughly 50% more likely to miss her if the identification is across races (e.g., a White person identifying an Asian person, or an Asian person identifying a Black person) than if it is within a race. Likewise, if the criminal is *not* present in the photospread, the risk of the witness falsely identifying someone who's actually innocent is roughly 50% higher in cross-race identification.

Why should this be? We have emphasized that the recognition system people use is configuration-based only when they are making an identification within an enormously familiar category—and the fact is that most people are extremely familiar with faces from their own race, less so with faces from other races. As a result, people can rely on the configuration-based mechanism when making same-race identifications, and so they benefit from this system's sensitivity and sophistication. When making cross-race identifications, however, people are less sensitive to the face's configuration. They therefore have to base their identification on the face's features, and it turns out that this is an appreciably less effective means of identifying individual faces. As a result, cross-race identifications end up being less accurate. Apparently, then, courts need to be especially cautious in interpreting cross-race identifications.

But does every witness show this pattern? Or, perhaps, is the disadvantage with cross-race faces smaller for people who live in a racially integrated environment?

Questions like these continue to be the subject of research, with some studies indicating that more contact between the races does, in fact, diminish the difference between same-race and cross-race identifications. However, the results of this research are uneven, making it unclear how (or whether) cross-race contact influences the effect. In the meantime, it's already clear that this issue may help the courts in deciding when to put full trust in a witness's identification and when to be wary of an identification's accuracy.

For more on this topic

Meissner, C. A., & Brigham, J. C. (2001). Thirty years of investigating the own-race bias in memory for faces: A meta-analytic review. *Psychology, Public Policy, and Law, 7*, 3–35.

Pezdek, K., Blandon-Gitlin, I., & Moore, C. (2003). Children's face recognition memory: More evidence for the cross-race effect. *Journal of Applied Psychology, 88*, 760–763.

Wright, D., & Stroud, J. (2002). Age differences in lineup identification accuracy: People are better with their own age. *Law and Human Behavior, 26*, 641–654.

FOR DISCUSSION

Right after a crime, police officers usually ask crime witnesses to *describe* the perpetrator. Then, days later, the police show the witnesses a *photo* of the alleged perpetrator, together with five other photos, and ask the witnesses to select the perpetrator from this group. Of course, witnesses vary in how accurate their verbal descriptions are, but—perhaps surprisingly—there is little relationship between how accurate the description is and the probability, later on, that the witness will make an accurate identification. Sometimes the description is wrong on many points, but the witness recognizes the perpetrator's photo anyhow; sometimes the description is relatively accurate, but the witness does not recognize the photo.

Given what you know about feature-based and configuration-based recognition, can you explain this pattern? Why isn't there a closer correspondence between the accuracy of the description and the likelihood of recognizing the photo? In addition, what is your hypothesis about how this pattern might change in cross-race identifications? In other words, we can, for *same-race identifications*, examine the relationship between (1) accuracy of verbal description, and (2) likelihood of accurately recognizing a photo; then we can examine the same relationship for *cross-race identifications*. Would you expect a difference? (In fact, evidence suggests there is indeed a difference here; can you figure out what it is?)

CHAPTER 4

Paying Attention

Demonstrations

4.1 Shadowing

For this demonstration, it will be best if you can work with another person, and even better if you can find two other people, so that the three of you can try out the various steps that are described below. If you can't find another person, you can use a voice on TV or radio, or any other sound recording of someone speaking.

Many classic studies in attention involved a task called *shadowing*. The instructions for this task go like this:

> You are about to hear a voice reading some English text. Your job is to repeat what you hear, word for word, as you hear it. In other words, you'll turn yourself into an "echo box," following along with the message as it arrives and repeating it back, echoing as many of the words as you can.

As a first step, you should try this task. You can do it with a friend and have him or her read to you out of a book, while you shadow what your freind is saying. If you don't have a cooperative friend, try shadowing a voice on a news broadcast, a podcast, or any other recording of a voice speaking in English.

Most people find this task relatively easy, but they also figure out rather quickly that there are adjustments they can make to make the task even easier. One adjustment is to shadow *in a quiet voice*, because otherwise your own shadowing will drown out the voice you're trying to hear. Another adjustment is in the *rhythm* of the shadowing: People very quickly settle into a pattern of listening to a phrase, rapidly spewing out that phrase, listening to the next phrase, rapidly spewing it out, and so on. This pattern of phrase-by-phrase shadowing has several advantages. Among them, your thinking about the input as a series of *phrases* (rather than as individual *words*) allows you to rely to some extent on *inferences* about what is being said—so that you can literally get away with listening less, and that makes the overall task of shadowing appreciably easier.

Of course, these inferences, and the whole strategy of phrase-by-phrase shadowing, depend on your being able to detect the *structure* within the incoming message—

and so this is another example in which your perception doesn't just "receive" the input; it also *organizes* the input. How much does this matter? If you have a cooperative friend, you can try this variation on shadowing: Have your friend read to you from a book, but ask your friend to read the material *backwards*. (So, for the previous sentence, your friend would literally say, "backwards material the read to friend your ask . . ."). This makes it much harder for you to keep track of the structure of the material—and therefore much harder to locate the boundaries between phrases, and much harder to make inferences about what you're hearing. Is shadowing of this backwards material harder than shadowing of "normal" material?

Now that you're practiced at shadowing, you're ready for the third step. Have one friend read normally (not backwards!) to you, and have a second friend read *something else* to you. (Ask the second friend to choose the reading, so that you don't know in advance what it is.) Again, if you don't have cooperative friends nearby, you can do the same with any broadcast or recorded voices. (You can play one voice on your radio and another from your computer, possibly relaying a podcast. Or you can have your friend do one voice while the TV news provides another voice. Do whichever of these is most convenient for you.) Your job is to shadow the first friend for a minute or so. When you're done, here are some questions:

- What was the second voice saying? Odds are good that you don't know.
- Could you at least hear when the second voice started and stopped? If the second voice coughed, or giggled, or hesitated in the middle of reading, did you hear that? Odds are good that you did.

In general, people tend to be oblivious to the *content* of the unattended message, but they hear the physical attributes of this message perfectly well—and it's that pattern that we need to explain. The textbook chapter walks through exactly the theories you'll need to explain these observations.

4.2   Automaticity and the Stroop Effect

For this demonstration, you will need to refer to Figure 4.4 in the textbook and Figure 13 in the color insert.

As the textbook chapter describes, actions that are well practiced can become automatic, and this automaticity has advantages and disadvantages. On the positive side, automatic actions can be done easily and without much attention, allowing you to focus on other concerns. On the negative side, automatic actions are difficult to control. (In fact, these observations are linked: Automatic actions become easy because you're no longer taking steps to control them.)

The classic demonstration of automaticity is the Stroop effect, described in the text. However, even though the chapter has warned you about this effect, you're still vulnerable to it.

For example, as rapidly as you can, scan down the left column of Figure 4.4 and say out loud how many characters there are in each row. Then do the same with the right column. You'll probably find that it's much harder to do this with the right-hand column because you find yourself *reading* the numerals rather than *counting* them—and so "four" in response to "4 4," when you should say "two" (because there are two items in the row). In this case, the automatic nature of reading makes it very difficult *not* to read.

The classic version of this effect, though, involves colors; to see this, turn to Figure 13 in the color insert. The figure shows a series of letter strings, each printed in a certain ink color. Use a piece of paper to cover the letter strings, and then move the paper down the page, uncovering each string one by one. The moment each string comes into view, say out loud *the color of the ink—that is, the color that the letters are printed in.* Ignore the letters themselves; it does not matter for your purposes what the letters are.

The letter strings are all in one of these colors: red, blue, green, yellow, or black. Try to respond quickly, naming the ink color as rapidly as you can. Can you do it?

What did you say when you saw "red" printed in blue? Did you say "blue" (as you should have), or did you read the word? Likewise for the other color names?

In this version of the Stroop effect, we began with neutral items (strings of *X*'s and *Y*'s), rather than actual words. This was an effort to get you into a pace of rapid responding with no interference, so that when the key items (the word names themselves) arrived, you'd be unprepared and unguarded. Now that you've been through the list, though, you know exactly what's coming, so try the list again; this time you'll be prepared *and* guarded. As you'll see, this will diminish the interference a little—but only a little!

4.3   Color-Changing Card Trick

The phenomenon of "change blindness" is easily demonstrated in the laboratory, but also has many parallels outside of the lab. For example, many stage magicians rely on (some version of) change-blindness in their performances—with the audience amazed by objects seeming to materialize or dematerialize, or with an assistant mysteriously transformed into an entirely different person. In most of these cases, though, the "magic" involves little beyond the audience's failing to notice straightforward swaps that had, in truth, taken place right before their eyes.

A similar effect is demonstrated in a popular video on YouTube: www.youtube.com/watch?v=voAntzB7EwE. This demonstration was created by British psychologist Richard Wiseman, and you can also view it—and several other fun videos—on a Web site that Wiseman maintains: www.quirkology.com.

Watch the video carefully. Were you fooled? Did you show the standard change-blindness pattern: failing to notice large-scale changes in the visual input?

Notice also that you—like the audience at a magic performance—watched the video knowing that someone was trying to fool you with a switch that you would not notice. You were, therefore, presumably on your guard—extra-vigilant, trying not to be fooled. Even so, the odds are good that you were still fooled, and this is by itself an important fact. It tells us that being extra careful is no protection against change-blindness, and neither is an effort toward being especially observant. These points are crucial for the stage magician, who is able to fool the audience despite its best efforts toward detecting the tricks and penetrating the illusions. But these same points tell us something about the nature of *attention*. It is not especially useful, it seems, just to "try hard to pay attention." Likewise, *instructions* to "pay close attention" can, in many circumstances have no effect at all. In order to promote attention, people usually need some information about what exactly they should pay attention *to*. Indeed, if someone told you, before the video, to pay attention to the key (changing) elements, do you think you'd be fooled?

Applying Cognitive Psychology

Research Methods: The Power of Random Assignment

Is it hazardous to talk on a cell phone while driving? Many people believe it is, and they point to evidence showing that people who use a cell phone while driving are more likely to be involved in accidents, compared to people who do not use a cell phone while driving. Perhaps surprisingly, this association—between increased accident risk and cell-phone use—stays in place even if we focus only on "hands-free" phones; apparently, the problem is the phone conversation itself. But we need to ask: Is this evidence persuasive?

Actually, this evidence is ambiguous—open to more than one interpretation. Being alert to this ambiguity is crucial for science, because if results can be interpreted in more than one way, then we can draw no conclusions from them. What is the ambiguity in this case? Perhaps talking on a cell phone while driving is distracting and increases the likelihood of an accident. But, as an alternative, perhaps the drivers who use cell phones while on the road are the drivers who were, from the start, less cautious or more prone to take risks. This lack of caution is why these people talk on the phone while driving, and it's also the reason why they're more often involved in accidents. Thus, cell-phone use and accidents go together, but not because either one causes the other. Instead, both of these observations (cell-phone use and having accidents) are the by-products of a third factor—being a risk-taker in the first place.

In technical terms, the problem here is that the people who drive while on the phone are a *self-selected group*. In other words, they decided for themselves whether they'd be in our "experimental group" (the cell-phone users) or our "control" group (people who don't use phones while they drive). And, presumably, people make this choice for some reason—they have some tendency or attributes at the start that lead them to the behavior of using the phone while driving. Of course, it might be these initial attributes, not the cell-phone use itself, that caused the observed outcome—the increased accident rate.

If we really want to examine the effects of cell-phone use on driving, therefore, we need to make sure that our "phone group" and our "no-phone group" are equivalent to begin with, before cell phones enter the scene. If we then discover that cell-phone use is associated with more accidents, we'd know that the cell phones are indeed at fault, and not some preexisting difference between the groups.

Psychologists usually achieve this matching of groups by means of *random assignment*. In our example, rather than allowing research participants to sort themselves into a group of phone users and a group of nonusers, the experimenters would assign them to one group or the other on some random basis (perhaps a coin toss). This wouldn't change the fact that some drivers are careful and others are not, or that some are more attentive than others. But our coin toss would ensure that careless drivers have an equal chance of ending up in the phone or no-phone group, and likewise for careful drivers, or risky ones. As a result, our two groups would end up matched to each other, with each group containing the same mix of different driver types.

Random assignment is one of the most important tools in a psychologist's research kit, ensuring that groups are matched before an experiment begins. That way, if the groups differ at the *end* of the experiment, we can be sure it's because of our experimental manipulation, and not because of some preexisting difference.

With all of this said, what about cell-phone use? The evidence suggests that talking on a cell phone while driving *is* dangerous, because of the distraction. The evidence comes from laboratory studies—because it would be unethical to require people to use phones while actually driving; this would put them in danger, so it is unacceptable as a research procedure! However, the studies use high-tech, extremely realistic driving simulators, and the data are clear: Phone conversations while driving do increase the risk of accidents. Hence there is an important message in these data—but it's not a message we can draw from the evidence mentioned at the start of this essay (the greater accident frequency among cell-phone users). That initial bit of evidence is ambiguous, for the reasons we've discussed here. The evidence we need for our conclusion comes from studies relying on random assignment, and these studies do tell us that even with other factors held constant, you shouldn't be conversing while you drive.

For more on this topic

Strayer, D. L., & Drews, F. A. (2007). Cell-phone-induced driver distraction. *Current Directions in Psychological Science, 16,* 128–131.

FOR DISCUSSION

Students who take Latin in high school usually get higher scores on the Scholastic Aptitude Test, and they usually get better grades in college. Many people conclude from this that students *should* take Latin in high school—the training in Latin apparently improves their academic performance. However, this conclusion is unwarranted, and the problem is a lack of random assignment. What exactly is the problem here? Why don't we have random assignment in this case? What specific problems does the self-selection produce? Finally, if we really wanted to find out if taking Latin improves academic performance, how could we use random assignment to develop a worthwhile experiment?

Cognitive Psychology and Education: ADHD

When students learn about *attention,* they often have questions about *failures of attention:* "Why can't I focus when I need to?" "Why am I so distracted by my roommate moving around the room when I'm studying?" "Why can some people listen to music while they're reading, but I can't?"

One question, however, comes up more than any other: "I" (or "my friend" or "my brother") "was diagnosed with attention-deficit disorder; what's that all about?" This question refers to a common diagnosis: attention deficit/hyperactivity disorder, or ADHD. This disorder is often diagnosed in young children (e.g., before age 8), but it can also be diagnosed at later ages. The disorder is characterized by a number of behavioral problems, including impulsivity, constant fidgeting, and difficulty in keeping attention focused on a task. Children with ADHD have trouble organizing or completing projects, and they are usually perceived to be intrusive and immature. These problems generally become less intense as the child grows older, but some symptoms can persist throughout the life span.

The diagnosis of ADHD is controversial. Many children who receive this diagnosis do seem to have a genuine disorder, with genetic factors playing a large role in producing the symptoms. Some critics argue, though, that in other cases the diagnosis is just a handy label for children who are particularly active, or for children who don't easily adjust to a school routine or a crowded classroom. Indeed, some critics suggest that ADHD is merely a convenient categorization for physicians or school counselors who don't know how else to think about an unruly or especially energetic child.

In those cases in which the diagnosis is warranted, though, what does it involve? As we describe in the textbook chapter, there are many steps involved in "paying attention," and some of those steps involve *inhibition*—so that we don't follow every stray thought, or every cue in the environment, wherever it may lead. For most of us, this is no problem, and so we easily inhibit our responses to most distractors. We're thrown off track only by especially intrusive distractors—such as a particularly loud noise, a stimulus that has special meaning for us, or a completely unexpected input.

Researchers have proposed, though, that people with ADHD may have less effective inhibitory circuits in their brains, and so they are far more vulnerable to momentary impulses and chance distractions. This is what leads to their scattered thoughts, their difficulty in schoolwork, and so on.

What can be done to help people with ADHD? One of the common treatments is *Ritalin*, a drug that is a powerful stimulant. It seems ironic that we'd give a stimulant to people who are already described as too active and too energetic, but the evidence suggests that Ritalin is effective in treating actual cases of ADHD—probably because the drug activates the inhibitory circuits within the brain, helping the child to guard against his or her wayward impulses.

However, we should probably not rely on Ritalin as our sole treatment for ADHD. One reason is the risk of overdiagnosis already mentioned; it is worrisome that this powerful drug may be routinely given to people—including young children—who don't actually have ADHD. In addition, there are various concerns about the long-term effects and possible side effects of Ritalin, and this certainly motivates us to seek other forms of treatment. Some of the promising alternatives involve restructuring of the environment: If children with ADHD are vulnerable to distraction, we can help them by the simple step of reducing the sources of distraction in their surroundings. Likewise, if people with ADHD are likely to be influenced by whatever cues they detect, we can perhaps surround them with helpful cues—reminders of various sorts of what they're supposed to be doing and the tasks they're supposed to be working on. These simple interventions do seem to be helpful—especially with adults diagnosed with ADHD.

Overall, then, our description of ADHD requires multiple parts. The diagnosis is probably used too often, and this is troubling, especially if it leads to overuse of powerful medication. But the diagnosis is genuine in many cases, and the problems involved in ADHD are real and serious. Medication can help, but even here there is a concern about the side effects of the medication. Environmental interventions can also help and may, in fact, be our best bet for the long term, especially given the important fact that in most cases the symptoms of ADHD do diminish as the years go by.

For more information on this topic

Barkley, R. A. (2004). Adolescents with ADHD: An overview of empirically based treatments. *Journal of Psychiatric Practice, 10,* 39–56.

Barkley, R. A. (2006). *Attention-deficit hyperactivity disorder: A handbook for diagnosis and treatment* (3ʳᵈ ed.). New York: Guilford Press.

Halperin, J. M., & Schulz, K. P. (2006). Revisiting the role of the prefrontal cortex in the pathophysiology of attention-deficit/hyperactivity disorder. *Psychological Bulletin, 132,* 560–581.

Cognitive Psychology and the Law: What Do Eyewitnesses Pay Attention To?

Throughout Chapter 4 in the textbook, we emphasized how little information people seem to gain about stimuli that are plainly visible (or plainly audible) *if they are not paying attention to these stimuli.* It's therefore crucial that we ask what eyewitnesses pay attention to during a crime. With that, what factors make it easier to pay attention? What factors distract the witness, so that he or she ends up noticing less and then reporting less in response to police questions?

One factor that seems crucial is the presence of a weapon. If, for example, a gun is on the scene, then of course witnesses will want to know whether the gun is pointed at them or not, whether the criminal's finger is on the trigger or not, and so on. After all, what else in the scene could be more important to the witness? But with this focus on the weapon, many other things in the scene will be unattended, so that the witness may fail to notice, and later on fail to remember, many bits of information crucial for law enforcement.

Consistent with these suggestions, witnesses to crimes involving weapons are sometimes said to show a pattern called *weapon focus.* They are able to report to the police many details about the weapon (e.g., its size, its color), and often many details about the hand that was holding the weapon (e.g., whether the person was wearing any rings or a bracelet). However, because of this focus, the witness may have a relatively poor memory for other aspects of the scene—including such forensically crucial information as what the perpetrator looked like. Indeed, studies suggest that eyewitness identifications of the perpetrator may be systematically *less accurate* in crimes involving weapons—presumably because the witness's attention was focused on the weapon, not on the perpetrator's face.

The weapon-focus pattern has been demonstrated in many studies, including those that literally track where participants are pointing their eyes during the event. Scientists have used a statistical technique called meta-analysis, providing an overall summary of these data, to confirm the reliability of this pattern and, importantly, to show that the weapon-focus effect is stronger and more reliable in those studies that are closer to actual forensic settings. Thus, the weapon-focus effect seems not to be a peculiar by-product of the artificial situations created in the lab; indeed, the effect may be *underestimated* in laboratory studies.

Somewhat surprisingly, though, it is difficult to document weapon focus in actual crimes. I testified once in a case involving a bank robbery; one witness offered a detailed description of the perpetrator's gun and the hand holding the gun, but then she said things that were plainly false about the perpetrator's face. (What she recalled was completely inconsistent with details that were visible on the videotape recorded by the bank's security system.) This certainly sounds like the pattern of weapon focus. But, in contrast, broader studies of actual police investigations usually show no evidence of weapon focus. Why is this? The answer may lie in the *duration* of the crime. A witness may focus initially on the weapon, but then, if the crime lasts long enough, the witness may have time to look at other aspects of the scene as well, decreasing the overall impact of the weapon-focus effect.

Even with this complication, demonstrations of the weapon-focus effect are important for many reasons, including the fact that they can help the courts in their evaluation of eyewitness testimony. After all, we obviously want to know when we can trust an eyewitness's recollection and when we cannot. To make these assessments, we need to know what factors shape a witness's memory, and it's on this basis that research on weapon focus can help us to evaluate each case, with the aim of maximizing the quality of courtroom evidence.

For more on this topic

Pickel, K. (2007). Remembering and identifying menacing perpetrators: Exposure to violence and the weapon focus effect. In R. Lindsay, D. Ross, J. Read, & M. Toglia (Eds.), *The handbook of eyewitness psychology: Vol. 2. Memory for people* (pp. 339–360). Hillsdale, NJ: Erlbaum.

Stanny, C. J., & Johnson, T. C. (2000). Effects of stress induced by a simulated shooting on recall by police and citizen witnesses. *American Journal of Psychology, 113*, 359–386.

Steblay, N. J. (1992). A meta-analytic review of the weapon focus effect. *Law and Human Behavior, 16*, 413–424.

FOR DISCUSSION

Can you generate other hypotheses about what people might pay attention to, during a crime, in addition to (or perhaps instead of) the weapon? Can you generate hypotheses about circumstances in which people are likely to focus their attention on details useful for the police, and circumstances in which they're unable to focus their attention (perhaps because they are so anguished over the crime itself)? The more we can specify what witnesses focus on, during a crime, the better position we will be in to ask what the witnesses will remember—and which aspects of their recollection we can count on.

The Acquisition of Memories and the Working-Memory System

Demonstrations

5.1 Primary and Recency Effects

The text describes a theoretical position known as the "modal model," in which working memory and long-term memory are distinct from each other, each governed by its own principles. A lot of the evidence for this distinction comes from an easily demonstrated data pattern.

Read the following list of 25 words out loud, at a speed of roughly one second per word. (*Before you begin,* you might start tapping your foot at roughly one tap per second, and then keep tapping your foot as you read the list; that will help you keep up the right rhythm.)

1. tree	8. kitten	15. strap	22. bell
2. work	9. view	16. bed	23. view
3. face	10. light	17. wheel	24. seat
4. music	11. page	18. paper	25. rope
5. test	12. truck	19. candle	
6. nail	13. lunch	20. farm	
7. window	14. shirt	21. ankle	

Now turn to the next page so you can't see this list anymore, and write down as many words from the list as you can in the box provided, in any order that you can.

Write down as many of the words from the list on p. 35 as you can recall here.

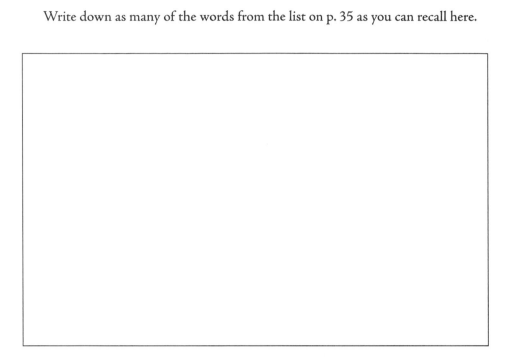

Compare your recall with the actual list. How many words did you remember? *Which* words did you remember? Every person will recall this list in a slightly different way, but there are several things that are likely to be true for your recall:

- Chances are good that you remembered the first three or four words on the list. Did you? The textbook chapter explains why this is likely.
- Chances are also good that you remembered the *final* three or four words on the list. Did you? Again, the textbook chapter explains why this is likely.
- Even though you were free to write down the list in any order you chose, it's very likely that you started out by writing the words you'd just read—that is, the *first* words you wrote were probably the *last* words you read on the list. Is that correct? The chapter doesn't explain this point fully, but the reason is straightforward. At the end of the list, the last few words were still in your working memory. If you then immediately thought about other words from the list, then these would enter working memory and so would *displace* from this memory the words you just heard; in that case, you might lose track of the words just read. To avoid this problem, you probably started your recall by "dumping" working memory's current contents (the last few words you read) onto the recall sheet. Then, with the words preserved in this way, it didn't matter if you displaced them from working memory, and this freed you to go to work on the other words from the list.

- Finally, it's likely that one or two of the words on the list really "stuck" in your memory, even though the words were neither early in the list (and so didn't benefit from *primacy*) nor late on the list (and so didn't benefit from *recency*). Which words (if any) stuck in your memory in this way? Why do you think this is? Does this fit with the theory in the text?

5.2   The Effects of Unattended Exposure

How does information get entered into long-term storage? One idea is that mere exposure is enough—so that if an object or scene is in front of your eyes over and over and over, you'll learn exactly what the object or scene looks like. However, this claim is *false*. Memories are created through a process of active engagement with materials; mere exposure is insufficient.

This point is easy to demonstrate, but for the demonstration you'll need to ask one or two friends a few questions. (You can't just test yourself because the textbook chapter gives away the answer, and so your memory is already altered by reading the chapter.)

Approach a friend who hasn't, as far as you know, read the *Cognition* text, and ask your friend these questions:

1. Whose head is on the Lincoln penny? (It will be troubling if your friend gets this wrong!)
2. Is the head facing forward, or is it visible only in profile? (Again, your friend is very likely to get this right.)
3. If the head is in profile, is it facing to the *right*, so that you can see the left ear and left cheek, or is it facing to the *left*, so that you can see the right ear and right cheek?

(For Canadian or British readers, you can ask the same questions about your nation's penny. Of course, your penny shows, on the "heads" side, the profile of the monarch who was reigning when the penny was issued. But the memory questions—and the likely outcome—are otherwise the same.)

Odds are good that half of the people you ask will say "facing right" and half will say "facing left." In other words, people trying to *remember* this fact about the penny are no more accurate than they would be if they answered at random.

Now, a few more questions. Is your friend wearing a watch? If so, reach out and put your hand on his or her wrist, so that you hide the watch from view. Now ask your friend:

4. Does your watch have all the numbers, from 1 through 12, on it? Or is it missing some of the numbers? If so, which numbers does it have?
5. What style of numbers is used? Ordinary numerals or Roman numerals?
6. What style of print is used for the numbers? An italic? A "normal" vertical font? A font that is elaborate in some way, or one that's relatively plain?

How accurate are your friends? Chances are excellent that many of your friends will answer these questions incorrectly—even though they've probably looked at their watches over and over and over during the years in which they've owned the watch.

In all of these cases, the explanation is straightforward. Information is not recorded in our memories simply because the information has been in front of our eyes at some point. Instead, information is recorded into memory only if we pay attention to that information and think about it in some way. People have seen pennies thousands of times, but they've not had any reason to think about Lincoln's position. Likewise, they've looked at their watches many, many times, but probably they've had no reason to think about the details of the numbers. As a result, and despite an enormous number of "learning opportunities," these unattended details are simply not recorded into memory.

Demonstration adapted from: Nickerson, R., & Adams, M. (1979). Long-term memory for a common object. *Cognitive Psychology, 11,* 287–307.

5.3   Depth of Processing

Many experiments show that "deep processing"—paying attention to an input's meaning, or implications—helps memory. In contrast, materials that receive only shallow processing tend not to be well remembered. This contrast is reliable and powerful, and also easily demonstrated.

On the next page is a list of questions followed by single words. Some of the questions concern categories. For example, the question might ask: "Is a type of vehicle? Truck." For this question, the answer would be yes.

Some of the questions involve rhyme. For example, the question might ask: "Rhymes with chair? Horse." Here the answer is no.

Still other questions concern spelling patterns—in particular, the number of vowels in the word. For example, if asked "Has three vowels? Chair," the answer would again be no.

Go through the list of questions at a comfortable speed, and say "yes" or "no" aloud in response to each question.

Rhymes with angle?	Speech	Rhymes with coffee?	Chapel
Is a type of silverware?	Brush	Has one vowel?	Sonnet
Has two vowels?	Cheek	Rhymes with rich?	Witch
Is a thing found in a garden?	Fence	Is a type of insect?	Roach
Rhymes with claim?	Flame	Has two vowels?	Brake
Has two vowels?	Flour	Has one vowel?	Twig
Is a rigid object?	Honey	Rhymes with bin?	Grin
Rhymes with elder?	Knife	Rhymes with fill?	Drill
Has three vowels?	Sheep	Is a human sound?	Moan
Rhymes with merit?	Copper	Has two vowels?	Claw
Rhymes with shove?	Glove	Is a type of entertainer?	Singer
Is a boundary dispute?	Monk	Rhymes with candy?	Bear
Rhymes with star?	Jar	Has four vowels?	Cherry
Has two vowels?	Cart	Is a type of plant?	Tree
Is a container for liquid?	Clove	Rhymes with pearl?	Earl
Is something sold on street corners?	Robber	Has two vowels?	Pool
Is a part of a ship?	Mast	Is a part of an airplane?	Week
Has four vowels?	Fiddle	Has one vowel?	Pail

This list contained 12 of each type of question—12 rhyme questions, 12 spelling questions, and 12 questions concerned with meaning. Was this task easy or hard? Most people have no trouble at all with this task, and they give correct answers to every one of the questions.

Each of these questions had a word provided with it, and you needed that word to answer the question. *How many of these "answer words" do you remember?* Turn to the next page, and write down as many of the answer words as you can.

List as many of the "answer words" as you can recall here:

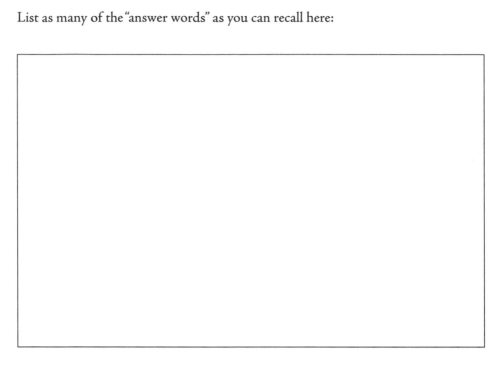

Now, go back and check your answers. First, put a check mark alongside of the word if it did in fact occur in the earlier list—so that your recall is correct.

Second, for each of the words you remembered, do the following:

Put an *S* next to the word you recalled *if* that word appeared in a spelling question (i.e., asking about number of vowels).

Put an *R* next to the word you recalled *if* that word appeared in one of the rhyming questions.

Put an *M* next to the word you recalled *if* that word appeared in one of the questions concerned with meaning.

How many *S* words did you recall? How many *R* words? *M* words?

It's close to certain that you remembered relatively few *S* words, more of the *R* words, and even more of the *M* words. In fact, you may have recalled most of the twelve *M* words; did you?

Is this the pattern of your recall? If so, then you just reproduced the standard level-of-processing effect, with deeper processing (attention to *meaning*) reliably producing better recall, for the reasons described in the textbook chapter.

Demonstration adapted from: Craik, F., & Tulving, E. (1975). Depth of processing and the retention of words in episodic memory. *Journal of Experimental Psychology: General, 104*, 269–294.

Applying Cognitive Psychology

Research Methods: Replication

In the Research Methods essays so far, we've talked about some of the steps needed to make sure an individual result from a particular experiment is unambiguous. We've talked about the need for a precise hypothesis, so that there's no question about whether the result fits with the hypothesis or not. We've talked about the advantages of random assignment, to make certain that the result couldn't be the product of pre-existing differences in our comparison groups. We've discussed the need to remove confounds so that, within the experiment, there is no ambiguity about what caused the differences we observe.

Notice, though, that all of these points concern the interpretation of individual results, so that each experiment yields clear and unambiguous findings. It's important to add, however, that researchers rarely draw conclusions from individual experiments, no matter how well designed the experiment is. One reason for this is statistical: A successful *replication*—a reproduction of the result in a new experiment—provides assurance that the original result wasn't just a fluke or a weird accident. Another reason is methodological: If we can replicate a result with a new experimenter, new participants, and new stimuli, this tells us there was nothing peculiar about these factors in the first experiment. This is our guarantee that the result was produced by the factors deliberately varied in the experiment and was not the chance by-product of some unnoticed factor in the procedure or the context.

In addition, researchers generally don't repeat experiments exactly as they were run the first time. Instead, replications usually introduce new factors into the design, to ask how these alter the results. (In fact, many scientific journals are hesitant to publish straight replications, largely because space is limited in the journals; however, the journals routinely publish studies that include a replication within a larger design that introduces new factors or new variations in addition to the replication.)

This broad pattern of "replication + variation" allows researchers to refine their hypotheses about a result, and also to test new hypotheses about the result. We gave one example of this approach in the textbook chapter: Specifically, if people are asked to recall as many words as they can from a list they just heard, the results show a characteristic U-shaped serial-position curve (see textbook, p. 137, Figure 5.2). This result is easily replicated, so we know it doesn't depend on idiosyncratic features of the experimental context—it doesn't depend on the specific words that are used in the procedure, or the particular group of participants we recruit, or the time of day in which we run the experiment. This allows us to move forward, asking the next question: What produces this reliable pattern? One proposal, of course, is provided by the *modal model,* a theoretical account of memory's basic architecture. But is this model correct?

To address this question, researchers have varied a number of factors in the basic list-learning experiment, factors that should, if the hypothesis is correct, alter the results. One factor is speed of list presentation: According to our hypothesis, if we slow down the presentation, this should increase recall for all but the last few words on the list. A different factor is distraction right after the list's end: Our hypothesis predicts that this will decrease the recency effect but will have no other effects. These predictions both turn out to be right.

Notice, then, that our claims about the modal model rest on many results, and not just one—in fact, this is the typical pattern in any science. Single results, on their own, are often open to more than one interpretation. Broad *patterns* of results, in contrast, usually allow just one interpretation—and that is what we want. Within the broad data pattern, some of the results show the replicability of the basic findings (e.g., the U-shaped data pattern). Other results provide tests of specific predictions derived from our model. In the end, though, it's the full fabric of results that tells us the model is correct, and it's this full fabric that tells us the model is powerful—able to explain a wide range of experimental data.

FOR DISCUSSION

As the textbook chapter describes, many studies show that someone's memory is improved if the person is led to do *deep and elaborate processing* of the material to be remembered. However, many of these studies test how well someone can memorize a list of words, and in our day-to-day lives we usually want to remember more complex, more interesting materials—such as complicated arguments or rich, many-part events. It's therefore important to test this hypothesis: "Instructions to do deep and elaborate processing also improve memory for complex materials, such as memory for an event."

Testing this hypothesis would, first of all, allow us to replicate the benefits of deeper processing; in this way, we could show that these benefits really are reliable. Testing this hypothesis would, in addition, allow us to extend our claims about deeper processing into a new arena. Can you design a study that would test this hypothesis?

Cognitive Psychology and Education: "How Should I Study?"

Chapter 5 discusses the ways new information gets established in memory. This is obviously relevant to the life of any student, who, after all, spends many hours of each day trying to gain new knowledge and skills, and hence is always trying to establish new information in memory.

What practical lessons can you as a student draw from Chapter 5? At the very least, the chapter makes it clear that you probably shouldn't spend much effort worrying about whether you'll remember the material or not, since we know that the intention to memorize contributes very little. Instead, you should focus your efforts on making sure you understand the material, because if you do, you're extremely likely to remember it.

As one way of working toward this understanding, you can often be well served by asking yourself, for each of the facts you learn: "Does this fact fit with other things

I know? Does this fact make sense? Do I know why this fact is as it is?" Seeking answers to these questions will promote understanding, which will in turn promote memory. In the same spirit, it is often useful to rephrase what is in your reading, or in your notes, in your own words—this will force you to think about what the words mean, which is a good thing for memory.

It is also useful to study with a friend—so that he or she can explain topics to you, and you can do the same in return. At the least, this will promote understanding, but it will also provide a different perspective on the materials being learned. And, of course, an additional perspective offers the possibility of creating new connections among ideas, and therefore new retrieval paths, making the information easier to recall later on.

Memory will also be best if you spread your studying out across multiple occasions—using what's called *spaced learning* (essentially, taking breaks between study sessions) rather than *massed learning* (essentially, "cramming" all at once). There are several reasons for this, including the fact that spaced learning makes it more likely that you'll take a slightly different perspective on the material each time you turn to it. This new perspective will allow you to see connections you didn't see before, and—again—the new connections create new links among ideas, which will provide retrieval paths that promote recall.

What about mnemonic strategies, like a peg-word system? These are enormously helpful—but only in some circumstances, and often at a cost. As the chapter mentions, focusing on the mnemonic may divert your time and attention away from efforts at understanding the material, and so you'll end up understanding the material less well. You will also end up only with the one or two retrieval paths that the mnemonic provides, and not the multiple paths created by comprehension. There are circumstances in which these drawbacks are not serious, and so mnemonics are often useful for remembering specific dates or place names, or particular bits of terminology. But for richer, more meaningful material, mnemonics may hurt you more than they help you.

Finally, let's emphasize that there's more to say about these issues, largely because our discussion in this essay has (like Chapter 5 itself) focused only on the "input" side of memory—getting information into "storage," so that it's available for use later on. As the chapter emphasizes, however, it may not be possible to separate these points about "input" from a consideration of the "output" processes (i.e., how you'll proceed when the time comes to *remember* this material). As one complexity, forms of learning that are effective for one sort of use may be less effective for other sorts of use, a complication that will be one of our main concerns in Chapter 6. As another complexity, we need to realize that the experience of being *tested* is both an "output" of previous learning and also a reencounter with the test materials, and so a refresher for those materials. This will be an important consideration in Chapter 7. Before we're done, therefore, we'll see that cognitive psychology can offer many lessons to the student—lessons concerned with a wide range of activities and strategies that can improve memory in classroom settings and beyond.

Cognitive Psychology and the Law:
The Videorecorder View

One popular conception of memory is sometimes dubbed the "videorecorder view." According to this view, everything in front of your eyes gets recorded into memory, much as a video camera records everything in front of the lens. This view, however, is wrong. As Chapter 5 of the textbook discusses, information gets established in memory only if you pay attention to it and think about it in some fashion. Mere exposure is not enough.

Wrong or not, the videorecorder view continues to influence how many people think about memory—including eyewitness memory. For example, many people believe that it is possible to hypnotize an eyewitness and then "return" the (hypnotized) witness to the scene of the crime. The idea is that the witness will then be able to recall minute details—the exact words spoken, precisely how things appeared, and more. All of this would make sense if memory were like a videorecorder. In that case, hypnosis would be akin to rewinding the tape and playing it again, with the prospect of noting things on the "playback" that had been overlooked during recording. However, none of this is correct. There is no evidence that hypnosis improves memory. Details that were overlooked the first time are simply not recorded in memory, and neither hypnosis nor any other technique can bring those details back.

Similarly, consider a technique often used in trials to raise questions about an eyewitness's recall. The attorney will ask the eyewitness question after question about an event and will quickly discover that the witness recalls some facts but not others. Later, the attorney is likely to ask the jury, "How can we trust this witness's recall? With so many gaps in the witness's recollection, it's clear that the witness was not paying attention or has a poor memory. We therefore cannot rely on what the witness says!"

However, the attorney's argument assumes the videorecorder view. If memory were like a videorecorder, then we *should* worry if the playback has gaps or errors in it. (If your actual videorecorder, or your DVD player, has gaps in its playback, skipping every other second or missing half the image, that surely does sound like a malfunction.) But this is not how memory works. Instead, memory is by nature selective. People recall what they paid attention to, and if a witness cannot recall some aspects of a crime, this merely tells us that the witness wasn't paying attention to everything. And, indeed, given what we know about the limits of attention, the witness probably *couldn't* pay attention to everything. Hence it is inevitable that the witness's memory will be selective, and we certainly must not use that selectivity as a basis for distrusting the witness.

Related examples are easy to find, cases in which popular ideas and often-used arguments rest on the (incorrect) videorecorder view. Once we understand how memory works, therefore, we gain more realistic expectations about what eyewitnesses will or will not be able to remember. With these realistic expectations, we are in a much better position to evaluate and understand eyewitness evidence.

To learn more on this topic:

Brewer, N., Potter, R., Fisher, P., Bond, N., & Luszcz, M. (1999). Beliefs and data on the relationship between consistency and accuracy of eyewitness testimony. *Applied Cognitive Psychology, 13,* 297–313.

Dywan, J., & Bowers, K. (1983). The use of hypnosis to enhance recall. *Science, 222,* 184–185.

Newman, A., & Thompson, J. (2001). The rise and fall of forensic hypnosis in criminal investigation. *Journal of the American Academic of Psychiatry and the Law, 29,* 75–84.

Steblay, N. M., & Bothwell, R. (1994). Evidence for hypnotically refreshed testimony: The view from the laboratory. *Law and Human Behavior, 19,* 635–651.

FOR DISCUSSION

If hypnosis is *not* the way to improve witnesses' memory, then what *is* the way? Are there steps we can take to help witnesses remember more? Alternatively, if we can't *improve* memory, can we at least find ways to *evaluate* witnesses to decide which ones are likely to have correct and complete memories, and which ones are likely to have partial or inaccurate memories? We will have more to say about these topics in upcoming textbook chapters, but several ideas about these points are already suggested by our discussion in the textbook's Chapter 5. In thinking this through, you might reflect on your own experiences: What do you think has helped you, in some circumstances, to remember more? You might also consider what *steps* or *activities* are helpful in encoding information into memory, and then think about how these steps or activities might be relevant to the circumstances of an eyewitness.

CHAPTER 6

Interconnections Between Acquisition and Retrieval

Demonstrations

6.1   Retrieval Paths and Connections

Often the information you seek in memory is instantly available: If you try to remember your father's name, or the capital of France, the information springs instantly into your mind. Other times, however, the retrieval of information is more difficult.

How well do you remember your life before college? Think back to the sixth grade: How many of your sixth-grade classmates do you remember? Try writing a list of all their names in the box below. Do it now, before you read any farther.

Now read the questions below.

- What house did you live in when you were in the sixth grade? Think about times that friends came over to your house. Does that help you remember more names?
- Were you involved in any sports in the sixth grade? Think about who played on the teams with you. Does that help you remember more names?
- Where did you sit in the classroom in sixth grade? Who sat at the desk on your left? Who sat at the desk on your right? In front of you? Behind? Does that help you remember more names?
- Did you ride the bus to school, or carpool, or walk? Were there classmates you often saw on your way to or from school? Does that help you remember more names?
- Was there anyone in the class who was always getting in trouble? Anyone who was a fabulous athlete? Anyone who was incredibly funny? Do these questions help you remember more names?

Chances are good that at least one of these strategies, helping you "work your way back" to the names, did enable you to come up with some classmates whom you'd forgotten—and perhaps helped you to come up with some names you hadn't thought about for years!

Apparently, these "extra" names were in your memory, even though you couldn't come up with them at first. Instead, you needed to locate the right *retrieval path* leading to the memory, the right *connection*. Once that connection was in your mind— once you were at the right "starting point" for the path—it led you quickly to the target memory. This is just what we would expect, based on the claims in the chapter.

6.2   Encoding Specificity

The textbook argues that the material in your memory is not just a reflection of the sights and sounds you have experienced. Instead, the material in your memory preserves a record of how you *thought about* these sights and sounds, how you interpreted and understood them. This demonstration, illustrating this point, is a little complicated because it has two separate parts. First you'll read a list of words (on p. 49). Then you should leave the demonstration and go do something else for 15 to 20 minutes. Run some errands, perhaps, or do a bit of your reading for next week's class. Then, second, your memory will be tested.

Here is the list of words to be remembered. For each word, a short phrase or cue is provided to help you focus on what the word *means*. Read the phrase or cue out loud, then pause for a second or so, then read the word, then pause for a second or so, to make sure you've really thought about the word. Then move on to the next. Ready? Begin.

A day of the week:	Thursday	A large city:	Tokyo
A government leader:	King	A sign of happiness:	Smile
A type of bird:	Cardinal	A student:	Pupil
A famous psychologist:	Skinner	A long word:	Notwithstanding
A menu item:	Wine	Has four wheels:	Toyota
A personality trait:	Charm	A part of a bird:	Bill
A vegetable:	Cabbage	A member of the family:	Grandfather
Associated with heat:	Stove	A happy time of year:	Birthday
A round object:	Ball	A part of a word:	Letter
Found in the jungle:	Leopard	A tool:	Wrench
A crime:	Robbery	Found next to a highway:	Motel
A baseball position:	Pitcher	A type of sports equipment:	Racket
Associated with cold:	North	Part of a building:	Chimney
Song accompaniment:	Banjo	Made of leather:	Saddle
Taken to a birthday party:	Present	A tropical plant:	Palm
A girl's name:	Susan	A synonym for "big":	Colossal
A type of footgear:	Boots	Associated with lunch:	Noon
A manmade structure:	Bridge	Part of the intestine:	Colon
A weapon:	Cannon		
A sweet food:	Banana		
An assertion of possession:	Mine		

Now, what time is it? Go away and do something else for 15 minutes, then come back for the next part of this demonstration.

Next, we're going to test your memory for the words you learned earlier. To guide your efforts at recall, a cue will be provided for each of the words. Sometimes the cue will be exactly the same as the cue you saw before, and sometimes it will be different. In all cases, though, the cue will always be closely related to the target word. There are no misleading cues.

Here are the cues; next to each cue, write down the word from the previous list that is related to the cue. Do not look at the previous list. If you can't recall some of the words, leave those items blank.

A facial expression: _____

A large city: _____

Associated with coal: _____

A fruit: _____

A weapon: _____

A card game: _____

Needed in snow: _____

A girl's name: _____

A grammatical tense: _____

A musical instrument: _____

Associated with cold: _____

An article of pottery: _____

A type of illegal activity: _____

Found in the jungle: _____

A social event: _____

A kitchen appliance: _____

A vegetable: _____

A small trinket: _____

An alcoholic beverage: _____

A famous psychologist: _____

A clergyman: _____

A member of royalty: _____

A day of the week: _____

A punctuation mark: _____

A time of day: _____

A synonym for "big": _____

Part of the hand: _____

Associated with horse: _____

Part of a building: _____

A type of noise: _____

A vacation rest-stop: _____

A tool: _____

A form of communication: _____

A special day: _____

A member of the family: _____

A month reminder: _____

A type of car: _____

A long word: _____

Found in the eye: _____

Here are the *answers*. Check which ones you got right.

A facial expression:	Smile	A member of royalty:	King
A large city:	Tokyo	A day of the week:	Thursday
Associated with coal:	Mine	A punctuation mark:	Colon
A fruit:	Banana	A time of day:	Noon
A weapon:	Cannon	A synonym for "big":	Colossal
A card game:	Bridge	Part of the hand:	Palm
Needed in snow:	Boots	Associated with horse:	Saddle
A girl's name:	Susan	Part of a building:	Chimney
A grammatical tense:	Present	A type of noise:	Racket
A musical instrument:	Banjo	A vacation rest-stop:	Motel
Associated with cold:	North	A tool:	Wrench
An article of pottery:	Pitcher	A form of communication:	Letter
A type of illegal activity:	Robbery	A special day:	Birthday
Found in the jungle:	Leopard	A member of the family:	Grandfather
A social event:	Ball	A month reminder:	Bill
A kitchen appliance:	Stove	A type of car:	Toyota
A vegetable:	Cabbage	A long word:	Notwithstanding
A small trinket:	Charm	Found in the eye:	Pupil
An alcoholic beverage:	Wine		
A famous psychologist:	Skinner		
A clergyman:	Cardinal		

These words are obviously in groups of three, and the groups actually indicate three different types of cue. For the *second* word in each group ("Tokyo," "Cannon," etc.), the cue is *identical* to the cue you saw on the very first list. How many of these (out of 13) did you get right?

For the *first* word in each group ("Smile," "Banana," etc.), the cue is *closely linked* to the one you saw at first ("A sign of happiness" was replaced with "A facial expression," and so on). How many of these (out of 13) did you get right?

For the *third* word in each group ("Mine," "Bridge," etc.), the cue actually *changed the meaning* of the target word. (On the first list, "Bridge" was "A manmade structure," not "A card game;" "Racket" was "A type of sports equipment," not "A type of noise.") How many of these (out of 13) did you get right?

Most people do best with the *identical* cues and a little worse with the *closely linked* cues. Most people recall the fewest words with *changed-the-meaning* cues. Is this the pattern of your data?

These results fit with what the chapter describes as encoding specificity. What goes into your memory is not just the words; what goes into memory is more specific than that—the words *plus* some idea about their context. If that context changes, then the cue may not make adequate contact with what's in your memory; as a result, the cue will fail to trigger the memory—even if you're trying to recall something relatively recent.

Demonstration adapted from: Thieman, T. J. (1984). Table 1, A classroom demonstration of encoding specificity. *Teaching of Psychology, 11* (2), 102. Copyright © 1984 Routledge. Reprinted by permission from the publisher (Taylor & Francis Group, http://www.informaworld.com).

6.3   Priming Effects

Imagine that yesterday you read a particular word—"couch," for example. This encounter with the word can change how you react to the word when you see it today. This will be true even if your memory contains no explicit record of yesterday's event, so that you have no conscious memory of having read that particular word. Even without an explicit record, your unconscious memory can lead you to interpret the word differently the next time you meet it, or it can lead you to recognize the word more quickly. Implicit memories can also change your *emotional* response to a word. The emotional effect probably won't be enough to make you laugh out loud or shed a tear when you see the word, but it may be enough to make the word seem more attractive to you than it would have been without the priming.

These implicit memory effects are, however, difficult to translate into quick demonstrations, because the demonstrations are likely to leave you with both an implicit *and* an explicit memory of the stimulus materials, and the explicit memory will overshadow the implicit memory. In other words, if an experience does leave you with an explicit memory, this record might lead you to overrule the implicit memory. Thus, your implicit memory might pull you toward a particular response, but your explicit memory might allow you to refuse that response and lead you to a different one instead—perhaps a response that's not even close to the one favored by the implicit memory.

We can, however, demonstrate something close to these effects. For example, write a short sentence using each of the following words.

Wind	Bottle	Close
Read	Record	Refuse
Dove	Foot	Desert
Pet	Tear	Lead

It turns out that several of these words can be used in more than one way or have more than one meaning. (Think about how the "wind" blows and also how you "wind" up some types of toys.) How did you use these items in your sentences? It turns out that this use is guided by your memory: If you recently read a sentence like "He dove into the pool," you're more likely to use "dove" to indicate the activity rather than the bird. This effect will work even if you didn't especially notice the word when you first saw it, and even if, now, you have no conscious recollection of recently seeing the word. In other words, these priming effects depend on implicit memory, not explicit.

It turns out that the opening paragraphs of this demonstration used the word "read" in the past tense, priming you to use the word in the past tense. Did you, in your sentence? The paragraphs also primed you to use "record" as a noun, not a verb; "tear" as the name for the thing that comes out of your eye, not an action; "close" as an adjective, not a noun; and "refuse" as a verb, not a noun. You were also primed by the opening paragraphs to think of "lead" in the present tense (so that it rhymed with "seed").

Did the priming work for you, guiding how you used the test words in the sentences you composed? Did you notice the primes? Did you remember them? We should note, though, that these priming effects don't work every time, simply because a number of other factors, in addition to priming, also influence how you use these words. Even so, the probability of your using the word a certain way is certainly changed by the prime, and so most people do show these priming effects.

Applying Cognitive Psychology

Research Methods: Double Dissociations

The textbook chapter describes a number of results showing that *implicit* memories are different from *explicit* ones. Thus, for example, certain forms of brain damage disrupt explicit memory but leave implicit memory intact. Likewise, we know that explicit memory is strongly influenced by level of processing during encoding, whereas implicit memory may not be. How should we think about findings like these?

It turns out that these results are ambiguous, and the ambiguity leads us to an important methodological issue. On the one side, we can read these results as suggesting that implicit memory is fundamentally different from explicit memory—governed by its own principles and served by separate portions of the brain. But on the other side, perhaps implicit and explicit memory are not different types at all. Perhaps they are fundamentally the same, obeying the same rules and principles. In that case, the memories we call "explicit" might simply be a more fragile version of this single type of memory, and hence they are more easily influenced by external factors such as brain damage or level of processing.

The issue at stake here is a crucial one that often arises in science: What is being asked, in essence, is whether the difference between the memory types is qualitative or quantitative, and it's important to get this straight. Claiming a *qualitative* difference is equivalent to claiming that the two are different "species" of memory. In that case, we will need different theories for implicit and explicit memory, and we'll confuse ourselves by classing the two types of memory together, seeking principles that apply to both. In contrast, claiming a *quantitative* difference is equivalent to saying the two are fundamentally similar, differing only in some "adjustment" or "parameter." In this case, we'd be wasting our time if we search for separate governing principles, because the same principles apply to both.

How can we resolve this ambiguity? The key lies in realizing that the facts we have mentioned so far (the effects of brain damage or of level of processing) are concerned with ways we can influence explicit memory with no effect on implicit. To demonstrate a qualitative difference, we also need the reverse result—cases in which we can influence implicit memory but not explicit. The moment we find such a result, we know that explicit memory is not just more fragile, or more easily influenced, than implicit memory—because sometimes, with some manipulations, it's implicit memory that's more easily influenced. As a consequence, we could no longer claim that either type of memory is weaker or more fragile than the other: Each type seems, in some experiments, to be the "stronger" memory (resistant to our manipulations) and seems, in other experiments, to be the "weaker." The only possible conclusion in this setting is that we can't talk about the two types in terms of which is stronger or weaker, more fragile or less; instead, we need to acknowledge that the two types are simply different from each other, each open to its own set of influences—and that is precisely the conclusion we are after.

This overall pattern of evidence—with some factors influencing one sort of memory but not the other, and some factors doing the reverse—provides what is called a *double dissociation,* and it allows us to rule out the possibility that explicit memories are simply more fragile than implicit (and hence more readily influenced by any manipulation). This in turn allows us to conclude that the difference is not just a quantitative one.

As the textbook chapter mentions, we do have the double dissociation for implicit and explicit memory: Certain factors (including forms of brain damage) influence explicit memory but not implicit; other factors (and other forms of brain damage) influence implicit memory but not explicit. Thus, neither type of memory is, in general, easier to influence than the other. This conclusion allows us to set aside the hypothesis that one of these types of memory is just a more fragile version of the other. Instead, the evidence tells us that each type of memory is indeed affected by its own set of factors. That tells us a lot about these forms of memory, but it also illustrates the power of a double dissociation.

In Chapter 5, we discussed the difference between *working memory* and *long-term memory*. These were two different types of storage, we argued, each with its own characteristics. Imagine, though, that someone offered an alternative view: "There's really just one type of memory. What we call 'working memory' is merely the information that's just arrived in memory, so that it's weaker, more easily disrupted, more likely to be forgotten, than memory that's been in storage for a longer time." This view suggests that the difference between (so-called) working memory and long-term memory is *not* a difference between types of memory; it is instead just a quantitative difference—a difference of "how much" (how strong, how long lasting) rather than a difference of "which type."

What evidence can you think of that speaks against this alternative view? Can we use the logic of a *double dissociation* here to show that working memory is not just weaker, shorter lasting, or more fragile but is instead truly different from long-term memory?

If you get stuck, think back to the basic logic of a double dissociation: Are there factors that influence working memory but not long-term memory? Are there are also factors that influence long-term memory but not working memory? If you can come up with factors of both sorts, this indicates that we can't just argue that one type of memory is "weaker" or "more easily disrupted" than the other—and that's the point.

Cognitive Psychology and Education:
Familiarity Is Potentially Treacherous

Sometimes you see a picture of someone and immediately say, "Gee—she looks familiar!" Your reaction to the picture seems to be a direct response to the stimulus itself, but the textbook chapter suggests that familiarity is far more complicated than this, and is the result of a many-step process. As a result of these complexities, a number of *errors* about familiarity are possible—including cases in which a stimulus feels familiar even though it's not, or cases in which you correctly realize that the stimulus is familiar but then make a mistake about *why* it's familiar.

These points highlight the dangers, for students, of relying on familiarity. As one illustration, consider the advice that people sometimes give for taking a multiple-choice test. They tell you, "Go with your first inclination" or "Choose the answer that feels familiar." In some cases these strategies will help, because sometimes the correct answer will indeed feel familiar. But in other cases these strategies can lead you astray, because the answer you're considering may seem familiar *for a bad reason:* What if your professor once said, "One of the common mistakes people make is to believe . . ." and then talked about the ideas summarized in the answer you're now considering? Alternatively, what if the answer seems familiar because it *resembles* the correct answer but is, in some crucial way, different from the correct answer and therefore mistaken? In either of these cases your sense of familiarity might lead you directly to a wrong answer.

As a different illustration, imagine the following scenario. You're talking with a friend, brainstorming about possible topics for a term paper you need to write. Your friend makes a suggestion, but you scoff at it because the idea seems too complicated. A few days later, you're again trying to think of topics for the paper, and the same idea pops into your thoughts. By then, you may have forgotten your conversation with your friend, and so you might have forgotten that your friend offered this very idea. But on this new consideration, the idea seems far more promising—perhaps because the exposure a week ago gave you some "warm-up" in thinking through the idea. As a result, you might now endorse the idea, and since you've forgotten your friend's suggestion, you might claim the idea as your own.

In fact, several studies have shown that this sort of *unconscious plagiarism* is relatively common. In this situation, the idea you're presenting as your own is, objectively speaking, familiar to you, thanks to your earlier conversation with your friend. However, the idea may not *feel* familiar. Thanks to the earlier encounter, you're now relatively fluent in your thinking about the idea, and this does make the idea feel special and distinctive. But (mistakenly) you don't interpret this specialness as familiarity; instead, you interpret it as an indication that the idea is especially clever. As a result—with no explicit memory of the earlier conversation with your friend, and with no sense of familiarity—you sincerely (but falsely) claim that the idea is yours.

What can you do to avoid these dangers—to avoid (in the multiple-choice case) the error of being misled by real familiarity, and to avoid (in the unconscious plagiarism case) the problem of *not detecting* an idea's familiarity? Perhaps the best answer is just to be alert to the complexities associated with familiarity. After all, you don't want to ignore familiarity, because sometimes it is helpful: Sometimes an option on a multiple-choice test seems familiar because it *is* the (correct) idea discussed in class. But given the difficulties we've mentioned here, it may be best to regard familiarity just as a clue about the past and not as an iron-clad indicator. That attitude may encourage the sort of caution that will allow you to use familiarity without being betrayed by it.

For more on this topic

Jacoby, L., & Hollingshead, A. (1990). Reading student essays may be hazardous to your spelling: Effects of reading incorrectly and correctly spelled words. *Canadian Journal of Psychology, 44,* 345–358.

Preston, J., & Wegner, D. M. (2007). The Eureka error: Inadvertent plagiarism by misattributions of effort. *Journal of Personality and Social Psychology, 92,* 575–584.

Stark, L.-J., Perfect, T., & Newstead, S. (2008). The effects of repeated idea elaboration on unconscious plagiarism. *Memory & Cognition, 36,* 65–73.

Cognitive Psychology and the Law:
Unconscious Transference

Imagine that you witness a crime. The police suspect that Robby Robber was the perpetrator, and so they place Robby's picture onto a page together with five other photos, and they show you this "photospread." You point to Robby's photo and say, "I think that's the guy, but I'm not at all sure." The police can't count this as a positive identification, but from other evidence they become convinced that Robby is guilty, and so he's arrested and brought to trial.

During the trial, you're asked to testify. During your testimony, the prosecutor asks, "Do you see the perpetrator in the courtroom?" When you answer yes, the prosecutor asks you to indicate who the robber is. You point to Robby and say, "That's the guy—the man at the defense table."

In-court identifications like the one just described are often persuasive for juries, but in truth, the identification just described is problematic for three reasons. First, research tells us that people are often better at realizing *that* a face is familiar than they are in recalling *why* the face is familiar. In the imaginary case just described, therefore, you might (correctly) realize that Robby's face is familiar and sensibly conclude that you've seen his face before. But then you might make an error about *where* you'd seen his face before, perhaps mistakenly concluding that Robby looks familiar because you saw him during the crime, when in actuality he looks familiar only because you'd seen his picture in the photospread! This error is sometimes referred to as *unconscious transference*, because the face is, in your memory, unconsciously "transferred" from one setting to another. (You actually saw him in the photospread, but in your memory you "transfer" him into the original crime—memory's version of a "cut-and-paste" operation.)

Second, notice that in our hypothetical case you had made a tentative identification from the photospread. You had, in other words, made a commitment to a particular selection, and research shows that the commitment can have powerful effects on subsequent identifications. In essence, it's very difficult to set aside your initial choice in order to get a fresh start in any later identification procedure. Thus, your in-court identification of Robby would be heavily influenced by your initial selection from the photospread—even if you made your initial selection with little confidence.

Third, in-court identifications are inevitably suggestive. In the courtroom, it is obvious from the seating arrangement who the defendant is. The witness also knows that the police and prosecution believe the defendant is guilty. These facts, by themselves, put some pressure on the witness to make an identification of the defendant—especially if the defendant looks in any way familiar.

How worried should we be about these three problems—the risk of unconscious transference, the effects of commitment, and the impact of a suggestive identification procedure? Research suggests that each of these can have a powerful effect on eyewitness identifications, potentially compromising in-court identifications. Indeed, some researchers would argue that even though in-court identifications are very dramatic, they are—because of the concerns discussed here—of little value as evidence.

In addition, note that some of these concerns also apply to out-of-court identifications. I testified in one trial in which the victim claimed that the defendant looked "familiar," and she was "almost certain" that he was the man who had robbed her. It turns out, though, that the man had an excellent alibi. What, therefore, was the basis for the victim's (apparently incorrect) identification? For years, the defendant had, for his morning run, used a jogging path that went right by the victim's house. It seems likely, therefore, that the defendant looked familiar to the victim because she had seen him during his run—and that she had then unconsciously (and mistakenly) transferred his face into her memory of the crime.

It's crucial, therefore, that the courts and police investigators do all that they can to avoid these various concerns. Specifically, if a witness thinks that the defendant "looks familiar," it's important to ask whether there might be some basis for the familiarity other than the crime itself. With steps like these, we can use what we know about memory to improve the accuracy of eyewitness identifications—and, in that way, improve the accuracy and the efficiency of the criminal justice system.

For more on this topic

Brown, E., Deffenbacher, K., & Sturgill, W. (1977). Memory for faces and the circumstances of encounter. *Journal of Applied Psychology, 62,* 311–318.

Davis, D., Loftus, E. F., Vanous, S., & Cucciare, M. (2008). "Unconscious transferrence" can be an instance of "change blindness." *Applied Cognitive Psychology, 22,* 605–623.

Dysart, J. E., Lindsay, R. C. L., Hammond, R., & Dupuis, P. (2001). Mug shot exposure prior to lineup identification: Interference, transference, and commitment effects. *Journal of Applied Psychology, 86,* 1280–1284.

FOR DISCUSSION

Can you think of examples from your own life in which you've experienced unconscious transference? This would include situations in which you were sure that you knew someone from one setting, when in fact you really had met the person in a completely different setting. Likewise, can you think of examples in which you realized that someone looked familiar, but you couldn't figure out *why* the person looked familiar? Is there some way we can communicate these examples to a jury, so that the jurors will make better use of identification evidence?

CHAPTER 7

Remembering Complex Events

Demonstrations

7.1 Associations and Memory Error

This is a test of immediate memory. Read List 1; then turn the page over and try to write down in the box, from memory, as many words as you can from the list. Then come back to this page, read List 2, turn the page over, and try to write down as many of its words as you can. Then do the same for List 3. When you're all done, read the material that follows.

List 1	List 2	List 3
Door	Nose	Sour
Glass	Breathe	Candy
Pane	Sniff	Sugar
Shade	Aroma	Bitter
Ledge	Hear	Good
Sill	See	Taste
House	Nostril	Tooth
Open	Whiff	Nice
Curtain	Scent	Honey
Frame	Reek	Soda
View	Stench	Chocolate
Breeze	Fragrance	Heart
Sash	Perfume	Cake
Screen	Salts	Tart
Shutter	Rose	Pie

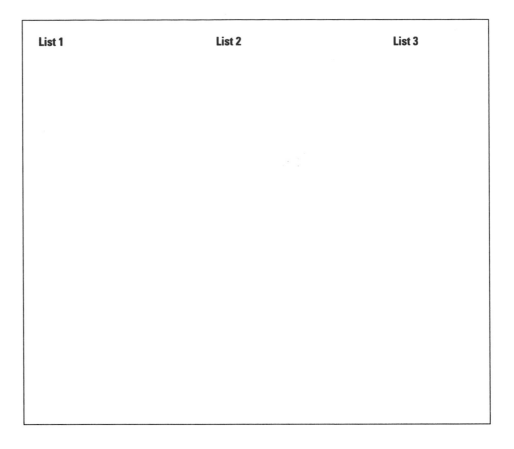

List 1	List 2	List 3

Don't read beyond this point until you've tried to recall each of the three lists!

Each of these lists is organized around a theme, but the word that best captures that theme is not included in the list. All of the words in List 1, for example, are strongly associated with the word "window," but that word is not in the list. All of the words for List 2 are strongly associated with "smell," and all in List 3 are strongly associated with "sweet," but again, these theme words are not in the lists.

In your recall of the lists, did you recall seeing "window" in List 1? "Smell" in List 2? "Sweet" in List 3?

This procedure is called the "DRM procedure," in honor of the researchers who have developed this paradigm (Deese, Roediger, and McDermott). In this situation, often half of the people tested do make these specific errors—and with considerable confidence. Of course, the theme words are associated with the list in your memory, and it is this association that leads many people into a memory error.

Demonstration adapted from: McDermott, K., & Roediger, H. (1998). False recognition of associates can be resistant to an explicit warning to subjects and an immediate recognition probe. *Journal of Memory and Language, 39,* 508–520. Also, Roediger, H., & McDermott, K. (1995). Creating false memories: Remembering words not presented in lists. *Journal of Experimental Psychology: Learning, Memory and Cognition, 21*(4), 803–814.

7.2   Memory Accuracy and Confidence

As you have seen, a large part of Chapter 7 is concerned with the errors people make when they are trying to recall the past. But how powerful are the errors? Here is one way to find out. In this demonstration, you will read a series of sentences. Be warned: The sentences are designed to be tricky and are similar to each other. Several of the sentences describe one scene; several describe other scenes. To make this challenging, though, the scenes are interwoven (and so you might get a sentence about Scene 1, then a sentence about Scene 2, then another about Scene 1, then one about Scene 3, and so on).

Try to remember the sentences—including their wording—as accurately as you can. Take this demonstration in a quiet setting, so that you can really focus on the sentences. Can you avoid making any mistakes?

To help you just a little, the memory test will come immediately after the sentences, so that there's no problem created by a long delay. Also, to help you even more, the memory test will be a *recognition* test, so that the sentences will be supplied for you, with no demand that you come up with the sentences on your own.

Finally, to allow you to do your best, the memory test won't force you into a yes-or-no format. Instead, it will allow you to express degrees of certainty. Specifically, in the memory test you'll judge, first, whether the test sentence was included in the original list or not. Second, you'll indicate how confident you are, using 0% to indicate "I'm really just guessing" and 100% to indicate "I'm totally certain." Of course, you can use values between 0% and 100% to indicate intermediate levels of certainty.

In short, this is a demonstration designed to ask *how good* memory can be—with many factors in place to support performance: ample warning about the nature of the materials; encouragement for you to give your best effort; immediate testing, via recognition; and allowing you to "hedge your bets" by expressing your degree of certainty. Can we, in these ways, document nearly perfect memory?

Here are the sentences to memorize. Read them with care, because they are tricky to remember.

1. The girl broke the window on the porch.

2. The tree in the front yard shaded the man who was smoking his pipe.

3. The hill was steep.

4. The cat, running from the barking dog, jumped on the table.

5. The tree was tall.

6. The old car climbed the hill.

7. The cat running from the dog jumped on the table.

8. The girl who lives next door broke the window on the porch.

9. The car pulled the trailer.

10. The scared cat was running from the barking dog.

11. The girl lives next door.

12. The tree shaded the man who was smoking his pipe.

13. The scared cat jumped on the table.

14. The girl who lives next door broke the large window.

15. The man was smoking his pipe.

16. The old car climbed the steep hill.

17. The large window was on the porch.

18. The tall tree was in the front yard.

19. The car pulling the trailer climbed the steep hill.

20. The cat jumped on the table.

21. The tall tree in the front yard shaded the man.

22. The car pulling the trailer climbed the hill.

23. The dog was barking.

24. The window was large.

Now, immediately go to the next page for the memory test.

For each of the sentences below, was the sentence on the previous list? If so, mark "Old." Or is this a new sentence? If so, mark "New." Also mark how confident you are, with 0% meaning "just guessing" and 100% indicating "totally certain." Remember, you can also use values between 0% and 100% to indicate intermediate levels of certainty.

Old ___ New ___ Confidence _____	The car climbed the hill.
Old ___ New ___ Confidence _____	The girl who lives next door broke the window.
Old ___ New ___ Confidence _____	The old man who was smoking his pipe climbed the steep hill.
Old ___ New ___ Confidence _____	The tree was in the front yard.
Old ___ New ___ Confidence _____	The scared cat, running from the barking dog, jumped on the table.
Old ___ New ___ Confidence _____	The window was on the porch.
Old ___ New ___ Confidence _____	The barking dog jumped on the old car in the front yard.
Old ___ New ___ Confidence _____	The tree in the front yard shaded the man.
Old ___ New ___ Confidence _____	The cat was running from the dog.
Old ___ New ___ Confidence _____	The old car pulled the trailer.
Old ___ New ___ Confidence _____	The tall tree in the front yard shaded the old car.
Old ___ New ___ Confidence _____	The tall tree shaded the man who was smoking his pipe.
Old ___ New ___ Confidence _____	The scared cat was running from the dog.
Old ___ New ___ Confidence _____	The old car, pulling the trailer, climbed the hill.
Old ___ New ___ Confidence _____	The girl who lives next door broke the large window on the porch.

How well did you do? This is the moment at which we confess that there is a trick here: *Every one of the test sentences was new.* None of the test sentences were identical to the sentences used in the original presentation.

For many of the test sentences, you probably (correctly) said "New" and were quite confident in your response. Which test sentences were these? Odds are good that you gave a high-confidence "New" response to a test sentence that *mixed together elements from the different scenes* (e.g., "The old man who was smoking his pipe climbed the steep hill"—it was the car, not the man, who was climbing the hill). These sentences didn't fit with your understanding of the scenes, and your ability to recall this understanding is excellent. On this basis, whenever a test sentence didn't fit with your understanding, whenever the sentence mixed the scenes together, you easily identified the sentence as "New." Said differently, you have an excellent memory for the *gist* of the earlier sentences, and so you effortlessly rejected any sentences that didn't fit with that (well-remembered) gist.

But for other test sentences, you probably said "Old" and may even have indicated 90% or 100% confidence that the sentences were wrong. Notice, as one implication of this point, that we cannot count on *confidence* as an indication of accurate memories. Even high-confidence recall can be wrong.

As a separate implication, notice how hard it is to remember a sentence's phrasing even in circumstances that are designed to *help* your memory. (Again, the testing was immediate. Recognition testing meant that you didn't have to come up with sentences on your own. You were warned that the test would be difficult. You were trying to do well.) Even in this setting, errors (including high-confidence errors) can occur.

Of course, one might argue that this is an acceptable pattern. After all, what you typically *want* to remember is the gist of a message, not the exact wording. Do you care whether you recall the exact phrasing of this paragraph? Or is it more important that you remember the point being made here? Nonetheless, there are situations in which you *do* want to remember the wording, and for that reason the results of this demonstration are troubling. There are also situations in which you might have misunderstood what you experienced, or your understanding might be incomplete. Those situations make it worrisome that what you remember seems to be dominated by your understanding, and not by the "raw materials" of your experience.

Demonstration adapted from: Bransford, J. (1979). *Human cognition: Learning, understanding and remembering,* 1E. Belmont, CA: Wadsworth. © 1979 Wadsworth, a part of Cengage Learning, Inc. Reproduced by permission. www.cengage.com/permissions

7.3   Childhood Amnesia

Each of us remembers many things about our lives—including episodes that we experienced just once, and also routine events that we experienced over and over (such as sitting in English class in the ninth grade, or being at a party with friends). There is, however, one well-documented limit on the memories we have.

Think back to something that happened when you were 10 years old. (It will probably help to think about what grade you were in and who your teacher was. Can you remember anything about that year?) How about when you were 9 years old? When you were 8? When you were 7? What is the *earliest event in your life* that you can remember?

Many people have trouble remembering events that took place before they were 4 years old or so. Very few people can remember events that took place before they were 3. This pattern is so common that it often gets a name— *childhood amnesia,* or sometimes *infantile amnesia*. Do you fit this pattern? Can you remember events from the first three years of your life? If you can, is it possible that you're not remembering the event itself, but instead remembering family discussions about the event? Or remembering some photograph of the event?

Several explanations have been offered for childhood amnesia, and probably each of the explanations captures part of the truth. One important consideration, though, hinges on the young child's understanding of the world. As the textbook chapter discusses, we typically remember events by associating them with other knowledge that we have. But, of course, this requires that you *have* that other knowledge, so that you can link the new information to it. Young children lack this other knowledge, and this makes it very difficult for them to establish new information in memory.

As a further exploration, you should ask some of your friends about the earliest events in their lives that they can remember. Several lines of evidence suggest that women can recall earlier life events than men, and that children who were quite verbal at an early age can recall earlier life events than children who were less verbal. Do these claims fit with your observations?

Applying Cognitive Psychology

Research Methods: External Validity

How accurately do eyewitnesses to crimes remember what they have seen? To find out, many researchers have run "crime-simulation studies" in which they show their participants brief videos depicting a crime, and then test the participants' memories for the video. But can we trust this research?

In these simulation studies, we can set things up in just the way we like. We can design the video so that it allows the comparisons crucial for our hypotheses. We can take steps to remove confounds from the procedure and use random assignment to make sure our groups are matched prior to the procedure. All of this preparation guarantees that our results will be unambiguous and informative.

But one thing about these studies is worrisome: The laboratory is in many ways an artificial setting, and it's possible that people behave differently in the lab than they do in other environments. In that case, the crime-simulation studies may lack *external validity*—that is, they may not reflect the real-world phenomena that ultimately we wish to understand. As a consequence, we cannot *generalize* the lab results to situations outside of the lab.

How do we decide whether a laboratory result is generalizable or not? One option is to compare the laboratory data with appropriately chosen field studies—for example, studies of actual witnesses to actual crimes. The field studies by themselves are often difficult to interpret. (We obviously can't arrange a crime to remove confounds from our comparisons, nor can we randomly assign witnesses to one condition or another. This means that the field studies by themselves often suffer from the ambiguities described in earlier Research Methods essays in this workbook.) Nonetheless, we can ask whether the field data are as we would expect, based on the laboratory findings. If so, this increases our confidence that the lab findings must be taken seriously.

In addition, we can, as a separate endeavor, examine specific hypotheses about external validity. For example, actual crime witnesses are likely to be angry or afraid during the crime, in contrast to lab participants, who remain entirely calm during an experimental procedure. Does this limit the generality of the lab findings? We can find out by suitable research—comparing the memories of people who are excited with those of people who are calm. In this way, we can ask how (or whether) we need to alter our claims in light of this contrast.

In the same vein, research participants come into the lab knowing that they are entering an environment in which an experiment will take place. Witnesses to crimes, in contrast, have no preparation; instead, the crime occurs as an awful surprise in the middle of their routine. Does this matter for memory? We can find out by comparing memory for surprising events with memory for anticipated events, and in this way ask how seriously we need to take this potential problem.

Thanks to inquiries like these, most researchers conclude that in fact we *can* make claims about real eyewitness reports based on laboratory findings. Of course, the laboratory is different from the setting of a crime, but evidence suggests that these differences do not change how the event is remembered—and maybe this should not be surprising. After all, it seems unlikely that people reserve a special set of cognitive processes for use in the lab, processes different from the ones they use in day-to-day life. But with or without this broad suggestion, it does seem that we can generalize from the lab data.

Let's emphasize, though, that the issue of external validity has to be taken seriously and has to be addressed in a compelling way before we can draw generalizations from our findings. Above all, though, let's note that questions about external validity are themselves scientific questions—questions to be settled by research—as we seek to determine whether our lab studies do or do not reflect the real-world phenomena we ultimately want to explain.

FOR DISCUSSION

In the laboratory, we can show research participants a video of a crime or a staged crime that either does or does not involve a weapon. As we mentioned in an earlier essay (see pp. 33–34), if a weapon is in view, the participants tend to focus their attention on it—with the result that they end up remembering a lot about the weapon itself, but less about other aspects of the crime. However, this *weapon-focus effect* is difficult to demonstrate in field studies. In several studies, researchers have gained access to police records of actual crimes, including crimes in which a witness (or the victim) has been asked to identify the suspect from a lineup. This allows us to ask: If the crime involved a weapon, is the witness less likely to make an identification? This is what we might expect, based on the laboratory data. After all, if the witnesses focused on the weapon, they were not focused on the perpetrator's *face*, and so they should have a less clear, less complete, less accurate memory for the face, and therefore should be less likely to make an accurate identification.

However, this is not what the data show. In several studies of police records, the likelihood of making an accurate identification has essentially been the same in crimes that *did* involve weapons and crimes that *did not*. This seems, therefore, to be a case in which we may not be able to make predictions about the "real world" based on lab data—the "real-world" studies do not show the weapon-focus effect, even though that effect is easily and reliably documented in the lab.

How should we think about this? What differences are there between the real-world crimes and the lab studies that could plausibly explain this contrast? What studies could you design to ask if the differences you've identified are, in fact, the actual source of this seeming data contrast?

For more on this topic

Pickel, K. (2007). Remembering and identifying menacing perpetrators: Exposure to violence and the weapon focus effect. In R. Lindsay, D. Ross, J. Read, and M. Toglia (Eds.), *The handbook of eyewitness psychology: Vol. 2. Memory for people* (pp. 339–360). Hillsdale, NJ: Erlbaum.

Cognitive Psychology and Education:
Remembering for the Long Term

One of the important topics within this chapter of the textbook concerns memory for the long term—our ability to recall things that we learned or experienced weeks ago—or months or even years ago. This sort of long-term retention is at the heart of autobiographical memory, because many of our personal memories involve events that took place many years ago. But long-term retention is also important in educational settings: Facts that you learned as an undergraduate may be crucial for some question on the exam you'll take to get into graduate school (the LSAT if you're headed for law school; the GMAT if you're thinking about business school, etc.). For that matter, information you gain as a student may be crucial for your professional work later in life. How, therefore, can we help people to remember things for the very long term?

The answer turns out to be straightforward: The key is simply to revisit what you've learned periodically, and even a very brief refresher can help enormously. In one study, for example, students were quizzed on little factoids they had learned at some prior point in their life. ("Who was the first astronaut to walk on the moon?" "Who wrote the fable about the fox and the grapes?") In many cases, the students couldn't remember these little facts, and so they were given a quick reminder. The correct answer was shown to them for 5 seconds, with just the instruction to look at the answer, because they'd need it later on. Nine days later, the students were asked the same questions; would the 5-second reminder help them then?

Without the reminder, participants couldn't recall these answers at all. But nine days after a quick reminder, they were able to remember roughly half the answers. This isn't perfect performance, but it's surely an enormous return from a very small investment. And it's likely that a *second* reminder a few days later, again lasting just 5 seconds, would have lifted their performance still further and allowed them to recall the items after an even longer delay.

A similar lesson emerged from a study mentioned in the textbook chapter— Linton's efforts toward remembering the events of her own life. As the chapter discussed, Linton periodically tested her own recollection and then sometimes, after a delay, would circle back and retest herself for the same target event. Notice, then, that the first test served to evaluate memory (did she remember or not?) and also served as a reminder—because the test provided Linton with an occasion to think once again about the earlier episode. We can then ask about the effects of this reminder by looking at her performance on the *second* test—when she circled back to think about the same event.

Linton's data suggest that the reminder provided by the first test had a huge impact. Without this reminder, Linton couldn't remember 32% of the events in her target set. *With* the reminder, though, the amount of forgetting was cut in half—to just 16%.

The implication for students should be clear. It really does pay to go back periodically and review what you've learned—including material you've learned earlier this academic year and also the material you learned in previous years. The review does not have to be lengthy or intense; in the first study described here, just a 5-second exposure was enough to decrease forgetting dramatically. In Linton's study, the simple experience of quizzing herself on the target events cut forgetting in half. Perhaps, therefore, you would be well served by summarizing your lessons on flash cards and rapidly reviewing the flashcards every month or two. As it turns out, using flash cards to learn the material in the first place is a bad bet, because (as we've seen) learning requires thoughtful and meaningful engagement with the materials you're trying to memorize, and running through a stack of flash cards probably won't promote that thoughtful engagement. But using flashcards may be an excellent way to review material that is already learned. The studies reviewed here (and other evidence as well) suggest that this is an easy, effective, and remarkably efficient way to hold onto what you've learned—for days, and probably months, and perhaps even decades after you've learned it.

For more on this topic

Berger, S. A., Hall, L. K., & Bahrick, H. P. (1999). Stabilizing access to marginal and submarginal knowledge. *Journal of Experimental Psychology: Applied, 5*, 438–447.

Butler, A., & Roediger, H. L. (2008). Feedback enhances the positive effects and reduces the negative effects of multiple-choice testing. *Memory & Cognition, 36*, 604–616.

Carpenter, S., Pashler, H., & Vul, E. (2007). What types of learning are enhanced by a cued recall test? *Psychonomic Bulletin & Review, 13*, 826–830.

Carpenter, S., Pashler, H., Wixted, J., & Vul, E. (2008). The effects of tests on learning and forgetting. *Memory & Cognition, 36*, 438–448.

Linton, M. (1982). Transformations of memory in everyday life. In U. Neisser (Ed.), *Memory observed: Remembering in natural contexts* (pp. 77–92). San Francisco: Freeman.

Cognitive Psychology and the Law: Jurors' Memory

Chapter 7 of the textbook covers many topics directly relevant to the question of what eyewitnesses to crimes can or cannot remember. But memory is also relevant to the courts for another reason: Members of a jury sit and listen to hours (and, sometimes, many days) of courtroom testimony. Then they move into the jury room, where, on the basis of their recollection of the testimony, they must evaluate the facts of the case and reach a verdict. But what if the jurors don't remember the testimony they have heard? In some jurisdictions, members of the jury are allowed to take notes during the trial; but in many jurisdictions, they are not. Perhaps we should worry, therefore, about *jurors'* memories just as much as we worry about *witnesses'* memories.

Jurors' memories are, of course, influenced by the same factors as any other memories. For example, we know in general that people try to fit complex events into a mental framework, or schema. Aspects of the event that fit well with this schema are likely to be remembered. Aspects that do not fit with the schema may be forgotten or remembered in a distorted form, so that the now-distorted recollection does fit with the schema. This pattern has been documented in many settings, and so it's not surprising that it can also be demonstrated in jurors.

In the opening phase of a trial, lawyers from each side present their own "story" about how the contested events actually unfolded. Jurors are supposed to give equal weight to both stories, the one offered by the prosecutor (or the lawyers for the plaintiff) and the one offered by the defense. In actuality, though, jury members often prefer one of these stories right from the start, and then they try to understand the trial evidence by thinking about how it fits into that story.

In a way, these stories about the case are helpful: It turns out that jurors remember more of the trial evidence if they have a story in mind from the trial's start. That's because they can fit the facts into the framework provided by the story as each new bit of evidence arrives. Likewise, jurors will remember more of the trial evidence if we make it easier for them to fit the evidence into a story. Concretely, they'll remember more if the trial evidence is presented in "story sequence"—first, the earliest events in the story; then, later events; and so on.

But there's also a downside: Once jurors have adopted a story about the trial, evidence that's consistent with the story is more likely to be remembered; evidence inconsistent with the story is often forgotten. In addition, jurors can sometimes "remember" evidence that actually wasn't presented during the trial but that is consistent with the story!

These findings are just what we'd expect, based on what we know about memory in other settings. But these facts are also troubling, because we would obviously prefer that jurors remember all the evidence—and remember it accurately. Perhaps, therefore, we should seek changes in courtroom procedures or in juror strategy so that, in the end, the jurors' verdict will be based on an unbiased and complete recollection of the trial evidence.

In addition, it's important to bear in mind that jurors work together, as a group, to reach their verdict. Perhaps, therefore, jury members can remind each other, during their deliberations, about points that some of them may have forgotten, and can correct each other's memory errors when they retire to the jury room to discuss the case. This happens to some extent, and so deliberation does seem to improve jurors' memory—but only to a small extent. Why small? In the jury room, the people most likely to speak up about the evidence are the people who are most confident that they recall the trial well. However, the textbook chapter discusses the fact that *confidence* in one's memory is not always an indication that the memory is accurate. Therefore, the people who speak up may not always be the ones who remember the evidence correctly.

Overall, then, it seems that memory research highlights juror memory as yet another arena in which errors are possible, and the research points to another topic on which efforts at improving the legal system might be enormously desirable.

For more on this topic

Pennington, N., & Hastie, R. (1992). Explaining the evidence: Tests of the story model for juror decision making. *Journal of Personality and Social Psychology, 62*, 189–206.

Pritchard, M., & Keenan, J. (2002). Does jury deliberation really improve jurors' memories? *Applied Cognitive Psychology, 16*, 589–601.

FOR DISCUSSION

In some jurisdictions, jurors are allowed to *take notes* during a trial to help them remember the trial evidence. In other jurisdictions, jurors are allowed to *ask questions* of the witness. (The jurors submit their questions to the judge, who screens them to make certain the questions are legally permissible; if they are, the judge reads the questions to the witness, who then answers.) In still other jurisdictions, the judge *gives the jury instructions,* before the trial even begins, about the legal issues that are in play and how the key legal terms are defined. (In most jurisdictions, though, these instructions come only at the trial's end, just before the jury begins its deliberation.)

Based on what we know about memory, which of these variations in procedure are likely to improve jurors' ability to remember the trial evidence? Based on what we know about memory, are there other steps we can (or should) take that would help jurors to remember the evidence?

CHAPTER 8

Associative Theories of Long-Term Memory

Demonstrations

8.1 Activation in Memory Search

This demonstration is designed to illustrate some crucial points about how activation spreads within the long-term memory network.

Take a piece of paper, and list all of the *men's first names* you can think of that are also *verbs*. For example, you can *Mark* something on paper; you shouldn't *Rob* a bank. If you're willing to ignore the spelling, you can *Neil* before the queen. How many other men's names are also verbs? Spend a few minutes generating the list.

How do you search your memory to come up with these names? One possibility is that you first think of all the men's names that you know, and then from this list you select the names that work as verbs. A different possibility reverses this sequence: You first think of all the verbs that you know, and from this list you select the words that are also names. One last possibility is that you *combine* these steps, so that your two searches go on in parallel: In essence, you let activation spread out in your memory network from the MEN'S NAMES nodes, and at the same time you let activation spread out from the VERBS nodes. Then you can just wait and see which nodes receive activation from both of these sources simultaneously.

In fact, the evidence suggests that the third option (simultaneous activation from two sources) is the one you use. We can document this by asking a different group of people just to list all the verbs they know. When we do this, we find that some verbs come to mind only after a long delay—if at all. For example, if you're just thinking of verbs, the verb "rustle" may not pop into your thoughts. If, therefore, you were trying to think of verbs-that-are-also-names by *first* thinking about verbs, and then screening these, you're unlikely to come up with "rustle" in your initial step (i.e., generating a list of verbs). Therefore, you won't think about "rustle" in this setting, and so you won't spot the fact that it's also a man's name ("Russell"). On this basis, this name won't be one of the names on your list.

The reverse is also true: If you're just thinking about men's names, the name "Russell" may not spring to mind, and so, if *this* is the first step in your memory search (i.e., first generate a list of names; then screen it, looking for verbs), then you won't come up with this name in the first place. Therefore, you won't consider this name, won't see that it's also a verb, and won't put it on your list.

It turns out, though, that relatively rare names and rare verbs *are* often part of your final output. This makes no sense if you're using a "two-step" procedure (first generate names, then screen them; or first generate verbs, then screen them) because the key words would never show up in the first step of this process. But the result does make sense if your memory search combines the two steps. In that case, even though these rare items are only weakly activated by the MEN'S NAMES nodes or only weakly activated by the VERBS nodes, they are activated perfectly well if they can receive energy from both sources at the same time—and that is why these rare items come easily to mind.

And, by the way, Americans *Bob* for apples at Halloween. Yesterday, I *Drew* a picture and decided to *Stu* the beef for dinner. I can *Don* a suit, *Mike* a speaker, *Rush* to an appointment, *Flip* a pancake, or *Jimmy* a locked door. These are just some of the names that could be on your list!

8.2   The Tip-of-the-Tongue Effect

In the simplest version of the associative network, activation flows wherever the connections lead. Therefore, if you've activated nodes that are well connected to some target nodes, then it's almost inevitable that activation will spread from this starting point to the target, and so the target should come swiftly to mind. However, things don't always work that smoothly—and this demands some sort of modifications of the simple network model.

One demonstration of this pattern concerns the tip-of-the-tongue effect: This term refers to cases in which you are sure you know a word but cannot, at that moment, think of the word. The word is on the "tip of your tongue," but it still won't come to mind. In these cases, you often can recall what letter the word starts with and roughly how long the word is (how many syllables), but still you can't think of the word itself.

In this situation, you've plainly activated nodes that are near the target node. (Otherwise, how would you know the starting letter or the syllable count?) You are strongly activating these nearby nodes as you pour your energies into trying to recall the elusive word. Nonetheless, activation fails to flow to the target node, and so—in a maddening fashion—the target word just won't come to mind.

Odds are good that you've already experienced the frustration of the tip-of-the-tongue state, but in case you have not, consider the following definitions. In each case, is the word or name in your vocabulary? If it is, can you think of the word? If the word *is* in your vocabulary but you *can't* think of it right now, can you recall what letter the word starts with? Can you remember how many syllables it has?

You may not know some of these terms at all; other terms will immediately spring to mind. But in at least some cases, you're likely to end up in the maddening state of having the word at the tip of your tongue but not being able think of it.

1. The aromatic substance found in the gut of some whales, valued in earlier years for the manufacture of perfumes.
2. A tube-shaped instrument that is rotated to produce complex, symmetrical designs, created by light shining through mirrors inside the instrument.
3. A structure of open latticework, usually made of wood, used as a support for vines or other climbing plants.
4. The legendary Roman slave who was spared in the arena when the lion recognized him as the man who had removed a thorn from its paw.
5. An infectious, often fatal disease, often transmitted through contaminated animal substances and sometimes transmitted, in powder form, as an agent in germ warfare.
6. The scholarly study of word origins and word histories.
7. The American magician who died in 1926, famous for his escapes from chains, handcuffs, straitjackets, and padlocked boxes.
8. People who explore caves as a hobby or sport.
9. An instance of making a discovery by lucky accident.
10. An instrument for measuring wind velocity.
11. An Oriental art form involving complex paper-folding.
12. The formal term for the collection and study of postage stamps and related material.
13. A word or phrase that reads the same way backward or forward (e.g., "Madam I'm Adam").
14. A building, usually stone, housing a large tomb or several tombs.

Turn to the next page to find out what the words are.

Here are the words.

1. Ambergris	8. Spelunkers
2. Kaleidoscope	9. Serendipity
3. Trellis	10. Anemometer
4. Androcles	11. Origami
5. Anthrax	12. Philately
6. Etymology	13. Palindrome
7. Houdini	14. Mausoleum

Demonstration adapted from: Brown, R., & McNeill, D. (1966). The "tip of the tongue" phenomenon. *Journal of Verbal Learning and Verbal Behavior, 5,* 325–337. *Also,* James, L., & Burke, D. (2000). Phonological priming effects on word retrieval and tip-of-the-tongue experiences in young and older adults. *Journal of Experimental Psychology: Learning, Memory and Cognition, 26,* 1378–1391.

8.3   Semantic Priming

As Chapter 8 describes, search through long-term memory relies heavily on a process of spreading activation, with currently activated nodes sending activation outward to their neighbors. If this spread brings enough activation to some new set of nodes, then those nodes will themselves become activated. This activation will call your attention to those nodes, and this brings into your thoughts the sought-after information. However, even if nodes do not receive enough activation to become activated themselves, the "subthreshold activation" still has important effects.

Here is a list of anagrams (words for which we've scrambled up the letters). Can you unscramble them to figure out what each of the words is?

MOUNNTIA	VWAE
AES	CORVIT
PLOTI	DLISNA
HRTIS	NOCAE

Did you get them all? Turn the page to see the answers.

The answers, in no particular order, are "sea," "shirt," "desert," "victor," "island," "mountain," "wave," "pilot," and . . . what? The last anagram in the list actually has two solutions: It could be an anagram for the boat used in North America to explore lakes and streams, or it could be an anagram for the body of water that sharks and whales and sea turtles live in.

Which of these two solutions came to your mind? The answer isn't self-evident. If you happen to be a devoted canoeist, for example, then "canoe" may have come rapidly in your thoughts. But the odds are good that "ocean" is the word that came to mind for you. Why is this? Several of the other words in this series ("sea," "desert," "island," "mountain," "wave") are semantically associated with "ocean." Therefore, when you solved these earlier anagrams, you activated nodes for these words, and the activation spread outward from there to the neighboring nodes—including, probably, OCEAN. As a result, the word "ocean" was already primed when you turned to the last anagram, making it likely that this word, and not the legitimate alternative, would come to your thoughts as you unscrambled NOCAE.

Applying Cognitive Psychology

Research Methods: Chronometric Studies

Our mental processes are usually quite fast, but even so, they do take a measurable amount of time. And, by scrutiny of these times, we can learn a great deal about the mind. This is why *chronometric* (time-measuring) *studies* play a key role in our science. In these studies, participants are asked a specific question in each trial, and we measure how long they need to respond; hence our data take the form of *response times* (RTs). However, we need to be clear on what response-time data really tell us.

Let's take as an example a lexical-decision task. In each trial of this task, a sequence of letters is presented, and the participant must decide whether the sequence forms a word or not. If it does, the participant presses one button; if not, then a different button. In this situation, the trials we're interested in are the trials in which the sequence does form a word; those trials tell us how rapidly the participants can "look up" the word in their "mental dictionary." Trials in which the letter sequences *aren't* words are not helpful for this question. Nonetheless, we need to include these nonword trials as *catch trials*. If we didn't, then the correct answer would be "Yes, this sequence is a word" on every trial. Participants would quickly figure this out and would shift to a strategy of hitting the "yes" button every time without even looking at the stimulus. To avoid this problem, we include nonwords as catch trials to make sure that participants take the task seriously.

What do response times in this task measure? On every trial of a lexical-decision task, participants must identify the letters on the screen and then attempt to look up this letter sequence in memory. Then, depending on what the memory search reveals, participants must reach a conclusion about whether the sequence forms a word or not, and then make the physical movement of pressing the appropriate button to indicate their response.

The response times we measure, therefore, reflect the total time needed for all of these steps, even though in truth we're only interested in a part of this sequence—namely, the time needed to locate the word in memory. In other words, the *total* time isn't useful for us, because it includes many elements that we really don't care about. How, then, can we isolate just that bit of the process that is of interest? Let's imagine a comparison between trials in which the target word has been primed and trials with no priming. Both types of trials include letter-reading; both include a decision that, yes, the stimulus is a word; both include the physical movement of a button press. Therefore, if we find *differences* between these two types of trials, the differences cannot be the result of these elements, because these elements are exactly the same in both types. Any differences, then, must be the result of the one stage that *is* different between the two types of trials—a memory look-up in the presence of priming, as opposed to a memory look-up without priming. By examining that difference, we can ask what the effect of priming is—and that, in general, is the key to chronometric studies. We are usually interested in the differences in response times between conditions, and not the absolute times themselves; these differences allow us to isolate (and thus to measure) the processes we want to study.

Clearly, then, some craft is involved in the design of chronometric experiments. We must arrange for the proper comparisons, so that we can isolate just the processes that we're interested in. But with the appropriate steps taken, chronometric studies can provide enormously useful information about memory, perception, imagery, and many other mental processes.

FOR DISCUSSION

Social psychologists argue that people are often influenced by *implicit associations*. For example, in our memories the representation for "secretary" is associated with the representation for "female," and so the moment we hear about a secretary, we are automatically primed to think about females—and thus to assume that a secretary will be a woman, rather than a man. Similar associations guide our thinking about other professions (e.g., the moment we hear about a doctor, we are primed to think about males) and about different racial or ethnic groups.

Can you design an experiment that might test this proposal? You probably want to rely on chronometric methods, and you might rely on the procedures used for lexical-decision tasks. Bear in mind that these procedures show us that activating, let's say, the nodes for BREAD causes activation to spread to the neighboring nodes, including the nodes for BUTTER. These procedures then provide a direct way of detecting this priming of the nodes for BUTTER. Can you adapt these procedures to study implicit associations?

You might also think about how these implicit associations influence us. If people start thinking "female" every time they hear about secretaries, or if they start thinking "violence" every time they hear about members of certain racial or ethnic groups, how will this influence their judgments or their behavior? And if these associations are part of the automatic (thus, inevitable) spread of activation within memory, people may be guided by these associations whether they want to be or not.

Cognitive Psychology and Education: Maximizing Interconnectedness

The textbook chapter discusses the importance of *fan* within the memory network, and it turns out that fan has an ironic implication: In some situations, there may be a cost to "knowing too much," and in those situations, new learning can actually lead to worse memory. To see this, let's start with the fact that whenever a node is activated, activation will spread out from this source to all of its associated nodes. If there are *many* associated nodes (a high degree of fan), then each will get just a small share of the outward-spreading activation. If there are only a few associated nodes (a low degree of fan), then there are fewer channels sharing the activation, and so each will get a larger slice of the total activation.

Now, let's translate this into concrete terms. Imagine that you know only one fact about, say, aardvarks. Perhaps all you know is that aardvarks have long noses. In this situation (illustrated in Panel A), it's inevitable that whenever you think about aardvarks, thoughts of long noses will come to mind, because all of the activation spreading out from the AARDVARK node will go to the LONG NOSES node. There is, quite simply, nowhere else for it to go.

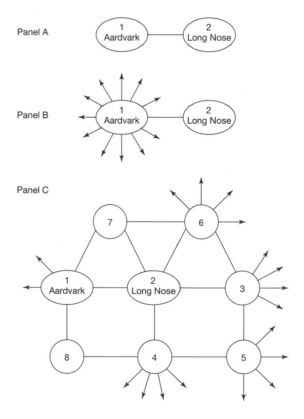

Things may go differently, though, if you learn some new (and independent) facts about aardvarks—if you learn that aardvarks are nocturnal, live in Africa, are closely related to elephant shrews, and have teeth with no enamel coating. In this case, your knowledge resembles the pattern shown in Panel B, with many nodes (each representing one of the new facts) radiating out from the AARDVARK node. In this case, when AARDVARK is activated, activation will spread to *all* of these associated nodes, and so each will receive just a small fraction of the total. As a result, it's possible that only a little activation will reach the node representing the fact about noses, and therefore this node may not itself become activated—effectively creating a situation in which your new learning has made it harder for you to remember the fact that you learned in the first place.

This is obviously an undesirable outcome—in which new learning makes old knowledge less accessible, as if the new learning were somehow undoing the old learning. How can you avoid this outcome? The answer is shown in Panel C. What you want to avoid is learning separate, independent facts about a topic. That's the scenario in Panel B, in which the new facts essentially compete with each other for activation.

What you want instead is to learn facts that are in many ways interconnected—in other words, you want to create the situation shown in Panel C. In this situation, the NOSE node still receives only a small share of the activation spreading outward from AARDVARK, but it can also receive activation from many other sources, and so, overall, it may be easier to activate the NOSE node in this situation than it would be in the situation shown in Panel B.

All of this creates a goal both for teachers and for students. It's probably a mistake for teachers to present their students with lists of facts or tables of information: "Here's a fact about aardvarks. . . . Here's another. . . ." (or: "Here's a fact about 17th-century Spain. . . . Here's another. . . ."). Instead, teachers need to put in the effort toward weaving these various facts into a coherent fabric, so that each fact can be understood through its connections with various other facts—actively working toward the situation shown in Panel C. (The same is true for anyone trying to present a series of facts—such as a trial attorney presenting facts for a jury to remember.)

From a student's perspective, the idea is similar. You put yourself at a disadvantage if you think of the material you're learning as providing a catalogue of separate bits, a listing of independent facts. Instead, you want to seek out points of connection among the various things you're learning. The connections may be thoughts about resemblance among different points, or thoughts about overlap, or about what's causing what, or about how *this* point might have been different if it weren't for *that* point. An effective teacher will guide you toward these connections, but you can't just rely on the teacher; you have to work on your own to weave the points together. This will ultimately improve your understanding; it will also, for the reasons we've sketched here, improve your memory; in particular, it will protect you from the bizarre situation (in Panel B) in which learning more leads you to remember less.

For more on this topic

Anderson, M. C., Bjork, R., & Bjork, E. (1994). Remembering can cause forgetting: Retrieval dynamics in long-term memory. *Journal of Experimental Psychology: Learning, Memory and Cognition, 20,* 1063–1087.

Anderson, M. C., Bjork, R. A., & Bjork, E. L. (2000). Retrieval-induced forgetting. Evidence for a recall-specific mechanism. *Psychonomic Bulletin & Review, 7,* 522–530.

Anderson, M. C., & McCulloch, K. C. (1999). Integration as a general boundary condition on retrieval-induced forgetting. *Journal of Experimental Psychology: Learning, Memory and Cognition, 25,* 608–629.

Van Overschelde, J. P., & Healy, A. F. (2001). Learning of nondomain facts in high- and low-knowledge domains. *Journal of Experimental Psychology: Learning, Memory and Cognition, 27,* 1160–1171.

Cognitive Psychology and the Law:
The Cognitive Interview

Police investigators must deal with the fact that eyewitnesses to crimes often fail to remember things that are crucial for an investigation—for example, facts that might help identify a perpetrator. Can we take any steps, therefore, to help witnesses remember more, to maximize the information we get from them? One promising approach is the *cognitive interview*. This technique has been developed by psychologists with the specific aim of improving eyewitness memory. Many studies suggest that this procedure does help both adult and child witnesses to remember more about an event; especially important, it does so without encouraging false memories. It is gratifying, then, that the cognitive interview has been adopted by a number of police departments as their preferred interview technique.

How does the cognitive interview work? Let's start with the fact that sometimes we cannot remember things simply because we didn't notice them in the first place, and so no record of the desired information was ever placed in long-term storage. In this situation, no procedure—whether it's the cognitive interview, or hypnosis, or simply trying really really hard to recall—can locate information that isn't there to be located. You cannot get water out of an empty bottle, and you cannot read words off a blank page. In the same fashion, you cannot recall information that was never placed in memory to begin with.

In many other cases, though, the gaps in our recollection have a different source: retrieval failure. The desired information *is* in memory, but we're unable to find it. In the terms we used in Chapter 8 of the textbook, activation does not reach the relevant nodes, and so those nodes aren't activated, and thus the desired information is never located. To *improve* memory, therefore, we need to increase the likelihood that the activation will reach the target nodes, and this is exactly what the cognitive interview tries to do.

As one aspect of the cognitive interview, the witness is encouraged to think back to how he felt at the time of the crime, and what the physical setting was like, and the weather. In other words, the witness is encouraged to reconstruct the environmental and physical context of the event, so that in essence he will put himself (during the interview) into the same frame of mind that he was in during the crime itself. This *context reinstatement* can improve memory in many situations for reasons we describe in the chapter: By putting someone back into the same mental context that he was in during the target event, we are likely to activate thoughts and ideas that are associated with that context. Activation can then spread from the nodes representing these ideas to the target materials.

In the cognitive interview, witnesses are also encouraged to approach the event they're trying to remember from more than one perspective, so that, for example, they're encouraged to recount the event from its start to its end, and then in reverse sequence from the end back to the beginning. This procedure also helps, and the reason is straightforward: By approaching the target memory from several different perspectives, we're providing multiple retrieval cues. Each cue will trigger its own nodes, sending activation to neighboring nodes. Each cue, therefore, can become a source of activation in memory; with many cues (i.e., many sources), we introduce a lot of activation into the network. If we choose our cues carefully—so that there's a reasonable likelihood that each cue might be connected to the target information—we maximize the chances of getting activation to the target, allowing memory retrieval. Even if each individual cue is, on its own, ineffective, the cue can still help us. That's because with multiple cues activated, it's likely that the target nodes in memory will receive activation from several sources at the same time, making retrieval much more likely.

Overall, then, it's no surprise that the cognitive interview is effective; the interview simply capitalizes on mechanisms that we already know to be helpful. More important, though, the cognitive interview provides a clear example of how we can use what we know about memory to aid anyone—including law enforcement professionals—who needs to draw as much information from memory as possible.

For more on this topic

Davis, M. R., McMahon, M., & Greenwood, K. M. (2005). The efficacy of mnemonic components of the cognitive interview: Towards a shortened variant for time-critical investigations. *Applied Cognitive Psychology, 19*, 75–93.

Fisher, R., & Schreiber, N. (2007). Interview protocols to improve eyewitness memory. In R. Lindsay, D. Ross, J. Read, & M. Toglia (Eds.), *Handbook of eyewitness psychology; Vol. 1. Memory for events* (pp. 53–80). Hillsdale, NJ: Erlbaum.

Holliday, R. E., & Albon, A. J. (2004). Minimising misinformation effects in young children with cognitive interview mnemonics. *Applied Cognitive Psychology, 18*, 263–281.

Koehnken, G., Milne, R., Memon, A., & Bull, R. (1999). The cognitive interview: A meta-analysis. *Psychology, Crime & Law, 5*, 3–27.

Milne, R., & Bull, R. (2002). Back to basics: A componential analysis of the original cognitive interview mnemonics with three age groups. *Applied Cognitive Psychology, 16*, 743–753.

FOR DISCUSSION

Based on the material in the chapter, are there other steps police officers should take to maximize what someone can recall? Are there steps that police officers should *avoid* taking to make sure they don't lead the witness in any way? In addition, can we carry these insights into other arenas? Imagine a physician trying to learn as much as possible about a patient's medical history; will the same procedures work there? Will the procedures need to be modified in any way? How about a newspaper reporter trying to write a story and needing information from witnesses to some newsworthy event? Will the procedures work in that case? Are any modifications needed?

CHAPTER 9

Concepts and Generic Knowledge

Demonstrations

9.1   Defining Concepts

The textbook chapter argues that people are typically unable to define their concepts—including concepts that they use all the time. Some concepts, though, do seem to have a firm definition. For example, what is a "bachelor"? According to most people, a bachelor is *an unmarried adult human male*. But does this definition really reflect the way people think about bachelors? For example, imagine that you were running an Internet match-making service, and you've decided to advertise your service to "bachelors." Which of the following men should receive your advertising?

- Alfred is an unmarried adult male, but he has been living with his girlfriend for the last 23 years. Their relationship is happy and stable. Should you send advertising to Alfred?

- Bernard is an unmarried adult male who does not have a partner. But Bernard is a monk, living in a monastery. Should you send advertising to Bernard?

- Charles is a married adult male, but he has not seen his wife for many years. Charles is earnestly dating, hoping to find a new partner. Should you send advertising to Charles?

- Donald is a married adult male, but he lives in a culture that encourages males to take two wives. Donald is earnestly dating, hoping to find a new partner. Should you send advertising to Donald?

Now, let's try a different perspective. Imagine that you work for the government, and you are trying to design a new set of tax laws. You believe that to make the law fair, people who are living with a partner, and perhaps supporting children, should be taxed differently from those who are only paying for their own expenses. For this reason, you want to define the term "bachelor" within the tax code, with the key idea being that a "bachelor" does not have a life-partner and (in most cases) does not have children. *For purposes of the tax law*, which of the four men, described earlier, should be counted as a "bachelor"?

As you read through the four examples, think about what it is that guides your judgments. The "guide" will, in part, involve your expectations about marriage and also society's rules for eligibility for marriage. You'll also want to think about the cultural setting (how common is it in our culture for bachelors to have children?). In light of these points, do you think that the term "bachelor" can be adequately represented in the mind by a clear definition? Can it be represented in the mind via a prototype or by some set of exemplars (with a random choice, on most occasions, for which exemplar you choose when you think about bachelors)? Or, perhaps, does this concept need to be represented by means of a network of beliefs, linking your idea of bachelor to your idea of marriage, family structure, and so on?

Demonstration adapted from: Fillmore, C. (1982). Towards a descriptive framework for spatial deixis. In R. J. Jarvella & W. Klein (Eds.), *Speech, place and action: Studies in deixis and related topics* (pp. 31–60). Chichester, England: Wiley.

9.2   Assessing Typicality

Many of the claims in Chapter 9 rest on the influence of typicality. But how do we assess typicality? In many experiments, participants have confronted an instruction like this:

> Some items of clothing are more typical of the category *clothing* than others. Rate each of the items below for how typical it is, using a "4" to indicate that the item is a highly typical item of clothing, and a "1" to indicate that the item is not at all typical. Use values in between to indicate intermediate levels of typicality.
> For each item, how typical is it?

Now, go ahead and rate the following items.

Shoes	Grass skirt	Gym shorts	Sari
T-shirt	Fedora	Socks	Top hat
Blue jeans	Pajamas	Sweatshirt	Stockings
Bathing suit	Belt	Leather pants	Miniskirt
Necktie	Ski boots	Mittens	Hawaiian shirt
Vest	Parka	Stole	Sweater
Underwear	Bra	Bathrobe	Dress shirt

Next, read the list to a friend and collect your friend's ratings of typicality. How much do you and your friend agree in your ratings? As you'll see, you and friend probably agree to an impressive extent. Apparently, therefore, typicality judgments aren't random or idiosyncratic. Instead, these judgments are a systematic reflection of the world in which we live—sometimes reflecting *frequency of encounter* (thus, clothing items that you often think about are counted as typical), and sometimes reflecting *beliefs* about what's central or important for the category.

Of course, you and your friend may disagree on some items. Can you find any pattern to the disagreement? If there is a pattern, will it lead us to alter our notion of what typicality is?

9.3   Basic-Level Categories

It is possible to categorize almost any object in several different ways. Right now, are you looking at a book? Or a college book? Or a cognitive psychology college book? Or is it just an "information source," or even a "physical object"? All of these labels are sensible, but which is the preferred label?

Spend a minute or so listing all of the traits you can think of that are *shared by all cars*.

Next, spend a minute or so listing all of the traits you can think of that are shared *by all moving vehicles* (including normal cars but also electric cars, dog-sleds, garbage trucks, jets, and the U.S. space shuttle).

Next, spend a minute or so listing all of the traits you can think of that are *shared by all Japanese cars.*

Most people find the first task (*cars*) easier than the second (*moving vehicles*). This fits with Rosch's claim that there is a level of categorization that seems more natural—it is the level she calls the "basic level." The category *cars* is a basic-level category, and so all cars really do seem to be like each other in important ways; this is why it is relatively easy to come up with traits that are shared by all cars. The category *vehicles*, on the other hand, is a superordinate category—one that includes several different basic-level categories. Superordinate categories strike people as providing less natural groupings of objects, and items within such a category often seem somewhat different from each other. This is why it is harder to come up with traits that are shared by all vehicles.

The category *Japanese cars* is a subordinate category—just a part of the basic-level category *cars*. Subordinate categories are narrower (i.e., they contain fewer things), but despite this greater precision, a categorization at the subordinate level provides you with little new information that you didn't already have from the basic-level category. For the category *cars*, you probably were able to list many attributes. For the category *Japanese cars*, were you able to add any attributes other than "made by a Japanese company" and, perhaps "reputation for reliability"?

It seems, then, that we lose information if our categorization is too general (i.e., if it focuses on a superordinate category). But it's not the case that the best categorization is the one that's most specific. That's because we gain a lot of information (i.e., we can identify many common attributes) when we shift from a superordinate category (like *vehicle*) to a basic-level category (like *car*), but then we gain very little information if we try to use more specific categorizations.

Demonstration adapted from: Rosch, E., Mervis, C., Gray, W., Johnson, D., & Boyes-Braem, P. (1976). Basic objects in natural categories. *Cognitive Psychology, 3,* 382–439.

Applying Cognitive Psychology

Research Methods: Limits on Generalization

In laboratory procedures, we study a particular group of participants doing a particular task with a particular stimulus. As we've discussed, though, we hope that our results are *generalizable*—revealing patterns that will also apply to other participants, other tasks, and other stimuli.

The need for generalizability is important throughout psychology, but especially so in the study of concepts. That's because research in this area is aimed at developing theories about conceptual knowledge itself, rather than theories about how the knowledge happens to be used for some particular task. It's crucial, therefore, that our data patterns generalize across tasks, so that we obtain similar results no matter what the task is. That's why researchers interested in conceptual knowledge seek *convergent data*—data from diverse paradigms that all point toward (and so "converge on") the same theoretical claims.

However, having emphasized the importance of generalization, let's also note that limitations on a result's generality can be informative. For example, Chapter 9 of the textbook describes the many ways in which the use of conceptual knowledge is influenced by typicality. More typical members of a category are remembered more easily, verified more quickly, and so on. Thus, the effects of typicality do generalize across tasks. But as the chapter discusses, there are limits on these effects—so that some tasks seem not to be influenced by typicality. This is crucial information, because it indicates that people sometimes rely on other sorts of conceptual knowledge in addition to typicality.

In short, then, if we find no generalization from a result (so that the result only emerges with one specific procedure or just one stimulus), then the result is not very interesting. But if a result does generalize and then we find *boundaries* (i.e., limits) on that generalization, this provides useful information, indicating that our theory needs to include another mechanism or process.

In addition, sometimes our hypothesis *predicts* boundaries on generalization, and so we need to demonstrate those boundaries in order to confirm the hypothesis. For example, imagine that we found a patient who had suffered brain damage and who had difficulty in, say, judging which was a more typical animal—a dog or an ibex, a mouse or a unicorn. We might hypothesize that this patient had trouble with judging typicality, but how would we test this hypothesis? First, we would expect the patient to have difficulty with other tasks that also hinge on typicality. In other words, we'd expect the initial observation with this patient to generalize to other tasks. But, second, we would expect this patient to behave normally in tasks that *don't* involve typicality. Thus, we would expect limits on the generalization, and finding those limits would ensure us that our evaluation of this patient was correct.

To put this differently, our hypothesis for this patient was not that he or she was disrupted in some global way. Instead, our hypothesis was that a particular process was disrupted; to test this, we need to show both that tasks relying on the process were impaired, and that tasks not relying on the process weren't impaired. This would demonstrate a *selective deficit* (i.e., a limitation in abilities on some tasks but not others), just as our hypothesis suggested; in this way, a failure of generalization is a crucial part of testing our hypothesis.

In exactly the same fashion, we might hypothesize that typicality effects are the result of "mental shortcuts" we take when we are trying to reason quickly about a concept. This hypothesis would predict not only (1) that typicality effects *would* emerge in a variety of fast-paced tasks (and so we'd expect generalization), but also (2) that typicality effects *wouldn't* emerge in more careful reasoning. (Remember that the hypothesis specified a shortcut *when we are trying to reason quickly*.) So here, too, a failure to generalize (i.e., *not* observing typicality in slower-paced reasoning) would be an important part of testing our hypothesis.

FOR DISCUSSION

The textbook chapter argues that prototypes are an important part of our conceptual knowledge, but only *part*. That leads to the claim that we sometimes rely on prototypes and sometimes don't, and so we sometimes should be influenced by typicality (resemblance to the prototype) and sometimes we should not. Can you generate a hypothesis about *when* people are likely to rely on prototypes, and when not?

Do you think that *fast-paced reasoning* is the key, as the essay implies? Do you think that *motivation to be*

careful might be the key? How about *familiarity with the concept*, so that prototype use is more common with less familiar concepts? Do you think the *nature of the task* matters?

Once you've developed your hypothesis, design a test for the hypothesis. According to your hypothesis, what sorts of tasks (or what sorts of concepts) should show a typicality effect, and what sorts should not?

Cognitive Psychology and Education:
Learning New Concepts

We often talk about learning new concepts, but what exactly does this mean? What is it that you're learning when you learn a concept? The textbook chapter offers an answer to this question, and the answer has implications for what, and how, you should learn. As it turns out, though, the implications draw us back to a theme we've met over and over in the text—the importance of connections for establishing, for representing, and for using knowledge.

In your studies, you encounter many new terms, and the terms are often accompanied by definitions. As the chapter argues, though, human knowledge often goes beyond definitions. For many of the terms you use, you don't have a definition; in fact, a definition may not even exist. Even when you do know a definition, your use of the concept often relies on other information—including a prototype for that term, as well as a set of exemplars. In addition, your use of conceptual information routinely depends on your broader knowledge that links this concept to other things you know. The broader knowledge encompasses what the text calls your "theory" about that concept, a theory that (among other things) explains why the concept's attributes are as they are.

You use your theory about a concept in many ways. Whenever you rely on a prototype, you are in essence drawing conclusions from the *resemblance* between the prototype and the new case you're thinking about, but resemblance in turn depends on your theory: It's your theory that tells you which attributes to pay attention to, in judging the resemblance, and which to ignore. (And so, if you're thinking about computers, your knowledge of computers tells you that the *color* of the machine's case is irrelevant. If, in contrast, you're thinking about clothing, your knowledge in this domain tells you that color is often an important attribute.) Likewise, you draw on your theory to guide your *inferences* about a concept (allowing you to decide, for example, whether Chihuahuas have sesamoid bones, now that you know that wolves have sesamoid bones).

Notice, then, that learning a definition for some new concept is a good place to start, but only a start (as in: "Deconstructionist philosophy is . . ."). In addition, you should seek out some *examples* of the new concept (as in: "Some instances of deconstructionist philosophy are . . ."). You also want to think about what these examples have in common; that will help you develop a *prototype* for the category. Above all, though, you want to think about what makes these count as examples—what is it about them that puts them into the category? How are the examples different, and why are they all in the same category despite these differences? Are some of the qualities of the examples predictable from other qualities? What caused these qualities to be as they are?

These questions (or other questions like them) will help you to start building the network of beliefs that provide your theory about this concept. These beliefs will help you to understand the concept and to use the concept. But, as the chapter discusses, these beliefs are in some ways *part of* the concept—providing the knowledge base that specifies, in your thoughts, what the concept is all about.

In some ways, these points put an extra burden on you and on your teachers. It would be easier if the teacher could simply provide a crisp definition for you to memorize, and then you could go ahead and commit that definition to memory. But that's not what it means to learn a concept, and this strict attention to a definition will leave you with a conceptual representation that's not very useful, and certainly far less rich than you want.

Cognitive Psychology and the Law:
Defining Legal Concepts

In many court cases, jury members have two jobs to do. First, they need to listen to the trial testimony in order to figure out exactly what a defendant did. Second, they need to decide whether or not those actions fit into a certain category: "robbery," or "assault," or "harassment."

To help the jury in this task, the laws define each crime in precise terms—so that there is a clear and detailed definition of "robbery," a clear definition of "trespassing," and so on. Even with these definitions, though, juries regularly encounter ambiguous cases in which it's just not clear whether someone's actions fit the definition of a crime or not. At the least, this reminds us how difficult it is to find adequately clear, broadly useful definitions for our concepts, a point that was important in the textbook chapter. But, in addition, we need to ask: How do jurors proceed when they encounter one of these ambiguous cases?

It should not be surprising that in these ambiguous cases jurors rely on the same categorization strategies that they use in most other situations. For example, the chapter discusses the fact that people often have *prototypes* in mind for their various concepts, and they assess a new case by asking how closely it resembles that prototype. It turns out that jurors do the same in making legal judgments; thus, they're appreciably more likely to convict someone if the trial facts resemble their prototype for the crime—if the trial facts fit their notion of, say, a "typical rape" or a "typical hit and run violation." Of course, the jury's prototypes have no official status within the law; indeed, the prototypes are likely to be shaped as much by TV crime shows as they are by the official statutes. Nonetheless, the prototypes do influence the jury, and so legal judgments, like concept use in general, seem to be influenced by typicality.

In addition, we argued in the chapter that concept users often seem to have a theory in mind about why a concept is as it is, and they use the theory in reasoning about the concept. For example, the textbook used the example of someone jumping into a pool fully clothed. You're likely to categorize this person as a "drunk," not because the person fits your definition for being drunk or even fits your prototype, but instead because you have a set of beliefs about why people act the way they do and how drunks are likely to act. Based on those beliefs (i.e., based on your theory), you decide that drunkenness is the most plausible explanation for the behavior you just observed, and you categorize accordingly.

Again, it seems that people carry these categorization habits into the courtroom. For example, consider the crime of *stalking*. This crime is extremely difficult to define in a crisp way, and neither opinion surveys nor court cases have produced a clear definition. In some cases, people have been convicted of stalking another person because the jury heard evidence indicating directly that the defendant intended to cause fear in the person being stalked. In other cases, the jury had no evidence for intention but *inferred* the intention from the fact that the stalking behavior persisted over many episodes. In still other cases, the jurors were influenced by the fact that the defendant was a former intimate of the person being stalked, with the jury apparently believing that in many settings former lovers are more likely to be stalkers than strangers.

What binds together these elements of stalking? It seems certain that jurors are relying on a broad set of beliefs about stalking—including what stalking is likely to involve, and what motivates one person to stalk another. In this way, stalking seems to rely on an implicit theory just as other concepts do. We must acknowledge this if we are to decide what stalking is and whether a particular individual should be convicted of this crime.

For more on this topic

Dennison, S., & Thomson, D. (2002). Identifying stalking: The relevance of intent in commonsense reasoning. *Law and Human Behavior, 26,* 543–561.

Huntley, J., & Costanzo, M. (2003). Sexual harassment stories: Testing a story-mediated model of juror decision-making in civil litigation. *Law and Human Behavior, 27,* 29–51.

Smith, V. L., & Studebaker, C. A. (1996). What do you expect? The influence of people's prior knowledge of crime categories on fact-finding. *Law and Human Behavior, 20,* 517–532.

FOR DISCUSSION

Imagine that you're working for the Judicial Committee for your community. Try to write a definition of stalking that could be used in deciding whether someone is guilty of this crime or not. Make sure to "test" your definition by trying to imagine cases that, in your view, *should* count as stalking; do they fall within your definition? Also try to imagine cases that, in your view, *should not* count as stalking, even if they have some of the elements often associated with this crime. Are they (correctly) excluded by your definition?

Language

Demonstrations

10.1   Phonemes and Subphonemes

A *phoneme* is the smallest unit of sound that can distinguish words within a language. Notice, therefore, that not all sound differences are phonemic differences. For example, the word "bus" can be pronounced with a slightly longer [s] sound at the end, or with a slightly shorter [s]. Both of these pronunciations, however, still refer to the motor vehicle used to transport groups of people. The difference between the long [s] and the short [s] is a *subphonemic* difference—one that does not distinguish words within the language.

What counts as a subphonemic difference, however, depends on the language. To see this, imagine that you were going to say the word "key" out loud. Get your tongue and teeth in position so that you're ready in an instant to say this word—but then freeze in that position, as if you were waiting for a "go" signal before making any noise. Now, imagine that you were going to say "coo" out loud. Again, get your tongue and teeth in position so that you're ready to say this word. Now, go back to being ready, in an instant, to say "key." Now, go back to being ready, in an instant, to say "coo."

Can you feel that your tongue is moving into different positions for these two words? That's because, in English, the [k] sound used in the word "key" is pronounced differently from the [k] sound used in "cool," and so, to make the different sounds, you need to move your tongue into different positions (they differ in where the tongue makes contact with the roof of the mouth).

The difference between the two [k] sounds is subphonemic in English (and so it doesn't matter for meaning). However, this difference does matter in certain other languages, including several Arabic languages. In these languages, there are two [k] sounds, and changing from one to the other will alter the identity of the word being spoken, even if nothing else in the word changes. In other words, the difference between the two [k] sounds is phonemic in Arabic, not subphonemic.

These differences between languages actually change how we perceive sounds. Most English speakers cannot hear the difference between the two [k] sounds; for

Arabic speakers, the difference is extremely obvious. A related case is the difference between the starting sound in "led" and the starting sound in "red." This difference is phonemic in English, so that (for example) "led" and "red" are different words, and English speakers easily hear the difference. The same acoustic difference, however, is subphonemic in many Asian languages, and speakers of these languages have trouble hearing the difference between words like "led" and "red" or between "leaf" and "reef." It seems, then, that speakers of different languages literally hear the world differently.

Can you learn to control which [k] sound you produce? Once again, get your mouth ready to say "key" out loud, but freeze in place before you make any sound. Now, without changing your tongue position at all, say "coo" out loud. If you do this carefully, you will end up producing the [k] sound that's normally the start for "key," but you'll pronounce it with the "oo" vowel. If you practice a little, you will get better at this; and if you listen very carefully, you can learn to hear the difference between "coo" pronounced with this [k], and "coo" pronounced with its usual [k]. If so, you've mastered one small element of speaking Arabic!

How do people learn to hear these different sounds, and to produce them, all in line with the language they ordinarily speak? The answer, oddly enough, is that they *don't* learn. Instead, young infants just a couple of months old seem perfectly capable of hearing the difference between the two [k] sounds, whether they live in an English-speaking community or an Arabic-speaking community. Likewise, young infants a few months old seem perfectly capable of hearing the difference between "led" and "red," whether the infants are born in an English-speaking environment or in Tokyo. However, if a distinction is not phonemic in their language, the infants lose the ability to hear these differences. This is, in other words, a clear case of "use it or lose it," and so, in a sense, infants at (say) 3 months of age can hear and make more distinctions than infants at 10 or 11 months of age.

10.2 Patterns in Language

Chapter 10 argues that in many ways our language is *generative* (so that new forms can always be developed) but also *patterned* (as if there were certain rules governing which new forms would be acceptable). This is why you could produce the novel sentence "Comical cartons leap joylessly," but not the sequence "Leap cartons joylessly comical." But what is the nature of these rules?

For example, ask the following questions to a couple of friends:

- Imagine that a beaver has been gnawing on a tree. If you later should see the tree, you'll see the marks the beaver has left behind. Are these *tooth-marks* or *teeth-marks*?
- Imagine that a hundred field mice are living in a farm house. Is the house *mouse-infested* or *mice-infested*?

- Now, imagine that 50 rats have also moved into the farm house. Is the house now *rat-infested* or *rats-infested*?
- Or, if 4-year-old Connor has written on the wall with three pens, did he leave behind *pen-marks* or *pens-marks*?

For the first two questions, most people feel like they could go either way—*tooth-marks* or *teeth-marks*; *mouse-infested* or *mice-infested*. For the next two questions, though, people reliably reject one of the options and insist that the house is *rat-infested* and that Connor left *pen-marks*. Is this consistent with how your friends answered?

What's going on here? It turns out that these combinations follow a rule—one that governs how morphemes combine. In essence, the rules says that if a noun has an *irregular plural*, then it can be combined with other morphemes in either its plural form or its singular form. But if a noun has a regular plural, it can be combined with other morphemes *only* in the singular form.

Our point here, though, is not to explore this particular rule. (In fact, this rule is derived from other rules governing how morphemes combine.) Our point instead is that this regularity exists within English, even though most people don't realize that there's a regular pattern. Therefore, in following this rule, people are not relying on a role they're consciously aware of or a rule that someone has taught them. Nonetheless, it's a rule they have been following since they were 3 or 4 years old. This by itself makes it clear that language is in fact heavily patterned, and that a large part of what it means to "know a language" is to learn (and to respect) these patterns.

Demonstration adapted from: Gordon, P. (1986). Level-ordering in lexical development. *Cognition, 21,* 73–93.

10.3   Ambiguity

Language is a remarkable tool for conveying ideas from one person to another. Sometimes, however, the transmission of ideas doesn't work quite the way it should. In some cases, the sentences we hear (or read) are unclear or misleading. In other cases, the sentences we encounter are ambiguous, and so the meaning we draw from them may be different from the meaning that the speaker (or writer) intended.

Sometimes the ambiguity we encounter concerns just one word: If you hear "Sam is looking for the bank," do you think Sam is looking for the river's edge or a financial institution? Sometimes the ambiguity is tied to the sentence's structure: If you hear "I saw a man on a horse wearing armor," then who is wearing the armor? Is it the man or the horse?

Remarkably, though, ambiguity in language is often overlooked. That's because we are so skilled at picking up the intended meaning of the speaker that we don't even realize that there is another way we might have interpreted the words. This failure to detect ambiguity is usually a good thing, because we are not distracted or misled by misinterpretations. But the failure to detect ambiguity can sometimes be a problem. In many cases, for example, actual newspapers have printed headlines without realizing that there was more than one way to interpret the headline.

All of the following are actual headlines that were printed in real newspapers. In each case, can you find both ways to interpret each headline?

EYE DROPS OFF SHELF

KIDS MAKE NUTRITIOUS SNACKS

STOLEN PAINTING FOUND BY TREE

DEALERS WILL HEAR CAR TALK AT NOON

MINERS REFUSE TO WORK AFTER DEATH

MILK DRINKERS ARE TURNING TO POWDER

COMPLAINTS ABOUT NBA REFEREES GROWING UGLY

POLICE BEGIN CAMPAIGN TO RUN DOWN JAYWALKERS

GRANDMOTHER OF EIGHT MAKES HOLE IN ONE

HOSPITALS ARE SUED BY 7 FOOT DOCTORS

ENRAGED COW INJURES FARMER WITH AX

SQUAD HELPS DOG BITE VICTIM

HERSHEY BARS PROTEST

Applying Cognitive Psychology

Research Methods: Methodological Opportunism

In these Research Methods essays, we have said a lot about the logic of research—including the steps one must take to ensure that the data are unambiguous, and the steps one must take to test a specific hypothesis. We have put less emphasis on the actual procedures used in research and, with that, the nuts and bolts of how one sets up an experiment, how one actually collects the data, and so on. This is because psychologists rely on an enormous range of methods, with no method having special status or privilege. This makes it less important that you learn the details of how a particular procedure is implemented. What you really need to understand is the set of elements shared by all our methods—and that is why we've emphasized the *logic* of research, rather than the specific techniques.

The diversity of methods psychologists use is evident in all corners of our field, including the study of language. To underscore this point, it may be useful to catalogue a few of the various forms of evidence that are crucial in Chapter 10 of the textbook.

In testing hypotheses about language, some of the relevant data come from conventional laboratory procedures. We ask research participants, for example, whether pairs of speech sounds are alike or different, and we record their error rates, thus testing hypotheses about categorical perception. We present sentences to participants and measure how long the participants need to interpret each sentence. In this way, we can document that active sentences are typically easier to understand than passive sentences, and so on.

In addition, we also collect a different form of data: metalinguistic judgments about whether a particular word or phrase is "acceptable" or not. Thus, we learn that people regard "He saw the cow" as acceptable, but not "He saw cow the"; as the textbook chapter describes, judgments like these are crucial for our efforts toward understanding what each of us knows about the language that we use all the time. The chapter also considers evidence from studies of young children learning language, as well as studies of individuals who have suffered damage to brain areas crucial for language. Both sorts of evidence help us understand the biological basis for language and, in many cases, the degree to which language skill is made possible by a large and complex set of diverse processes and structures.

Researchers interested in language also make use of the tools of neuroscience—and so we can examine patterns of activation in the brain when someone is hearing speech, or reading, or thinking about an ambiguous word. This provides us with insights into how the brain supports language use; it also provides us with information about some of the components of language.

We can also derive insights by comparing languages to each other. This was, for example, crucial in our discussion of linguistic universals, which in turn provide important suggestions about the biological roots of language.

Finally, language researchers also make extensive use of computer models as a means of testing their theories. Thus, for example, claims about how language is acquired have been examined by computer programs designed to use some specific procedure for learning language. We can then use the success (or failure) of these programs as indications of whether those procedures are adequate or not.

Overall, it should be clear that this research draws on a highly diverse set of methods, and it would be foolish to claim that there is a "standard" or "correct" way to do research in this arena. Instead, in an opportunistic way, we accept our data from whatever source, whatever technique, we can find. In all cases, though, the study must be designed so that the data are unambiguous and so that our hypothesis is tested in a rigorous manner. This is why we've emphasized these latter points—and therefore the logic of research—throughout these essays.

FOR DISCUSSION

The methodological opportunism we have highlighted here is not limited to the study of language. In Chapter 1, for example, we emphasized the diversity of methods used to study working memory, and a similar diversity of methods can be documented for almost any topic, any chapter, in the textbook. As an exercise, you might think through the collection of evidence we reviewed in Chapter 6 when we discussed the interconnections between memory acquisition and memory retrieval, or the evidence we reviewed in Chapter 7 when we discussed memory for complex events. In either of those chapters, can you find a study that hinged on chronometric data? On memory accuracy? Can you find a study that examined the nature of memory performance—that is, the types of errors, as opposed to just the number of errors? Can you find a study that hinged on subjective judgments (such as "how familiar" a stimulus feels or "how confident" a person feels about a memory)? Can you find a study that hinged on neuroimaging data? On neuropsychological data, focused on a particular case of brain damage?

Working through these questions will both help you to review (and thus to remember) the earlier chapter and also provide a clear illustration that our science is, in fact, truly opportunistic in its methods.

Cognitive Psychology and Education: Writing

As a student you obviously need to learn a lot of new material, but you also need to do a lot of writing—to document what you've learned (e.g., on an exam or in a paper) and also as part of your scholarly activities (e.g., as you develop a new argument or defend a new thesis). Can cognitive psychology provide any help for you in your writing, helping you to write more clearly and more persuasively?

Some specific bits of advice are mentioned in the Cognitive Psychology and the Law essay for this chapter. We know, for example, that people usually have an easier time with active sentences than passive, and so (all things being equal) active sentences are preferable. We know that people approach a sentence with certain strategies (e.g., minimal attachment), and so sentences are easiest to understand if they are compatible with those strategies.

In addition, it's important to remember that many people *speak* more clearly than they *write*, and it is interesting to ask why this is so. One reason is *prosody*—the pattern of pitch changes, and pauses, that we use in speaking. These cannot be reproduced in writing—although prosodic cues can sometimes be mimicked by the use of commas (to indicate pauses) or italics (to indicate emphasis). These aspects of print can certainly be overused, but they are in all cases important, and writers should probably pay more attention to them than they do, in order to gain in print some of the benefits that (in spoken language) are provided by prosody. But how should you use these cues correctly? One option is to rely on the fact that as listeners and speakers we all know how to use prosodic cues, and when we write we can exploit that knowledge by means of a simple trick: Specifically, it often helps to try reading your prose out loud. If you encounter a comma on the page but you're not inclined, as a speaker, to pause at that moment, then the comma is probably superfluous. Conversely, if you find yourself pausing as you read aloud but there's no comma, then you may need one.

Another advantage of spoken communication, as opposed to written, is the prospect of immediate feedback. If you say something that isn't clear, your conversation partner may frown, or look confused, or say something to indicate misunderstanding. What can take the place of this feedback when you're writing? As one option, it's almost always useful to have someone (a friend, perhaps) read over your drafts; this peer-editing can often catch ambiguities, or absence of clarity, or absence of flow, that you might have missed on your own. Even in the absence of a peer-editor, you can gain some of the same benefits from, once again, reading your own prose out loud. Some studies suggest that reading your own prose out loud helps you to gain some distance from the prose that you might not have with ordinary (silent) reading, so that you can, at least in a rough way, provide your own peer-editing.

Finally, many people shift into a different style of expressing themselves when they are writing—perhaps because they are convinced that they need some degree of formality in their written expression; perhaps because they are anxious while writing, and this stiffens their prose; or perhaps because they are deliberately trying to impress the reader, and so they reach for more complex constructions and more obscure vocabulary. Whatever the reason for these shifts, however, they are often counterproductive and make one's writing less clear, and wordier, and stiffer, than one's ordinary (spoken) expression. Part of the cure here is to abandon the idea that complex and formal prose is better prose. And part of the cure—once more—lies in either peer-editing or reading aloud. In either case, the question to ask is this: Would you express these ideas more clearly, more simply, if you were *speaking* them rather than writing them? Often this, too, will lead you to better writing.

Will these simple suggestions improve every writer? Probably not. Will these suggestions take obscure, fractured prose and lift it to a level that makes you eligible for a Pulitzer Prize? Surely not. Even so, the suggestions offered here may well help you in some ways, and for anyone's writing, any source of improvement should be welcome!

For more on this topic

Oppenheimer, D. M. (2006). Consequences of erudite vernacular utilized irrespective of necessity: Problems with using long words needlessly. *Applied Cognitive Psychology, 20,* 139–156.

Cognitive Psychology and the Law: Judicial Instructions

In some countries—including the United States—court cases are often decided by juries, and of course most jurors are not lawyers, so they need to be instructed in the law. This is usually accomplished by the judge providing *jury instructions* as the last step of the trial—just before the jury begins its deliberation. The instructions in a typical case might include a reminder of the jury's overall task, the exact definition of the crime being considered, the elements that must be proved in order to count a person as guilty of that crime, and so on.

These instructions obviously need to be accurate, and so they must capture the precision and exact definitions involved in the law. But the instructions also need to be clear—so that ordinary jurors (often people with just a high school education) can understand and remember the instructions and be guided by the law in their deliberation. It turns out, however, that these two requirements are often in conflict with each other, and sometimes *perfectly precise language* is not the same as *clear and comprehensible language.* As a result, judicial instructions are often difficult to understand.

In fact, some studies suggest that over half of judges' instructions are misunderstood by jurors; in some cases, less than 10% of the instructions are still remembered by the jurors after a brief delay. The failure to understand instructions can be documented in college students who are given the instructions as part of an experiment, and in actual jurors who hear the instructions as part of a real trial. In some cases the misunderstandings concern subtle details, but in other cases jurors seem to misunderstand fundamental points about the law. For example, American law rests on the idea that someone is innocent until proven guilty and that the defendant must, in a criminal trial, be proven guilty beyond a reasonable doubt. There's room for discussion about what "reasonable doubt" means exactly, but the implication of this idea is very clear: When the jury is genuinely uncertain about the verdict, they cannot vote "guilty." Nonetheless, juries seem sometimes to misunderstand this point and seem to adopt a rule of "If in doubt, then be careful, and that means don't risk letting the defendant go free—and so, if in doubt, convict."

What can we do about this? Studies of language processing tell us that people understand more when *participating* in a conversation rather than merely *hearing* a conversation. It is troubling, therefore, that jurors are expected to sit passively as the judge recites the instructions; jurors are almost never allowed to ask questions during the instructions about things they do not understand. And if the jurors realize, during their subsequent discussion, that they didn't understand the instructions, there is often little they can do. Requests for clarification often result in the judge's simply repeating the same words that caused the confusion in the first place.

The instructions themselves are also a problem, but psycholinguistic studies provide guides for how the instructions can be simplified. For example, we know that people generally have an easier time understanding active sentences than passive ones, affirmative sentences rather than negative ones. We also know that sentence understanding often depends on certain strategies (e.g., minimal attachment); sentences are easier to understand, therefore, if they have a structure that is compatible with these strategies. Using principles such as these, a number of researchers have developed jury instructions that still reflect the law correctly but are much easier to understand.

Where does this leave us? It is of paramount importance that jurors understand the law; otherwise, the jury system cannot function properly. It is therefore worrisome that jury comprehension of their instructions is so limited. But it is encouraging that by using what we know about language processing, we can make easy adjustments to improve the situation markedly.

For more on this topic

Ellsworth, P. C., & Reifman, A. (2000). Juror comprehension and public policy: Perceived problems and proposed solutions. *Psychology, Public Policy, and Law, 6*(3), 788–821.

Lieberman, J., & Sales, B. (1997). What social science teaches us about the jury instruction process. *Psychology, Public Policy, and Law, 3,* 589–644.

FOR DISCUSSION

Researchers often want to ask whether juries understand the instructions they have received, but how should this understanding be evaluated? Is there a "correct way" to evaluate understanding? In truth, there are several different ways we might try to assess people's understanding of instructions, and we can also assess their understanding either immediately or after some delay.

Imagine that you wanted to carry out a study of jury instructions—perhaps with the goal of comparing two different versions of the instructions, to ask which version led to greater comprehension. First, what would your options be for various ways to measure jurors' understanding of the instructions? Second, what option would you prefer—what do you think is the best way to evaluate someone's understanding?

CHAPTER 11

Visual Knowledge

Demonstrations

11.1   Imaged Synthesis

There is no question that mental images provide a direct representation of what a form or object looks like, and this information about appearances can be a source of new discoveries. Indeed, the history of science, technology, and the arts is filled with examples of great discoveries or great inventions being "seen" in a mental image and only later translated into a concrete, external object or a formula or theory.

We can easily demonstrate a miniature version of this process, relying on a procedure that is often used in the laboratory to study image-based problem-solving. The procedure involves *imaged synthesis*.

- Imagine a capitalized letter *D*. Lay this image down on its back, so that the vertical side lies flat and the rounded side bulges upward. Underneath it, position a capital letter *J*, centered underneath the *D* and just touching the vertical side that is lying flat. What have you produced?

- Imagine the number 7. Make the diagonal line into a vertical. Move the horizontal line down to the middle of the vertical line. Now, rotate the figure 90 degrees to the left. What have you produced?

- Imagine the letter *B*. Rotate it 90 degrees to the left so that it's lying on its back. Put a triangle directly below it having the same width and pointing down. Remove the horizontal line. What have you produced?

- Imagine the letter *Y*. Put a small circle at the bottom of it. Add a horizontal line halfway up. Now, turn the figure upside down. What have you produced?

- Imagine the letter *K*. Place a square next to it on the left side. Put a circle inside of the square. Now, rotate the figure 90 degrees to the left. What have you produced?

- Imagine the letter *D*. Rotate it 90 degrees to the right so that the bulge of D is at the bottom. Put the number 4 above it. Now, remove the horizontal segment of the 4 that's to the right of the vertical line. What have you produced?

How many of these led you to recognizable forms? Did you find (in this sequence) the umbrella, the letter *T*, a heart, a stick figure of a person, a TV set, and a sailboat?

Most people find these exercises relatively easy, and this provides a compelling demonstration that people really can "inspect" their images to find new forms and can make unanticipated discoveries from their images.

One question still to be asked, however, is whether this sort of "image-based creativity" involves the same processes that great scientists, artists, and inventors use. This is surely a difficult question, but it is worth noting that the laboratory procedures involving imaged synthesis do sometimes produce discoveries that seem quite creative. For example, in one study, participants were told to use these forms in any way they liked to produce something interesting or useful: a capital *P*, the number 8, and a capital *T*. One participant combined these forms to produce this snapshot of a croquet game:

Apparently, then, imaged synthesis in the lab can produce interesting sparks of creativity!

Demonstration adapted from: Reprinted from *Cognitive Science*, Vol. 13, Issue 1, January–March 1989, Ronald A. Finks, Steven Pinker, Martha J. Farah, "Reinterpreting Visual Patterns in Mental Imagery," pp. 51–78, Table 2, Copyright © 1989 Elsevier Science, Inc., with permission from Elsevier.

11.2   Mnemonic Strategies

Mental imagery plays a central role in many mnemonic strategies, including the peg-word systems we discussed in the textbook's Chapter 5. To see how this works, first you need to memorize the peg words themselves. Then, you'll "hang" the words you're trying to remember onto these "pegs."

We need to begin, therefore, with the peg words. Read the following rhyme (which you first met in Chapter 5) out loud twice; that will probably be enough for you to memorize the rhyme.

One is a bun.	Six are sticks
Two is a shoe.	Seven is heaven.
Three is a tree.	Eight is a gate.
Four is a door.	Nine is a line.
Five is a hive.	Ten is a hen.

1. The first peg is "bun," and the first word you want to memorize is "ashtray." What you need to do, therefore, is to "hang" this word on the peg. To do this, form some sort of mental picture that involves a *bun* and an *ashtray*. You can make the picture silly if you like, or give it some private meaning. (No one will ask you about your picture!) The key, though, is to make certain that the *bun* and the *ashtray* are not just side-by-side in the picture, but are somehow related to each other.

2. Now, do the same for the second peg, "shoe," and the next word to be memorized: "firewood." Form some mental picture that links a *shoe* and some *firewood*.

3. The next word to memorize is "picture." Form some mental picture that links a *picture* with the third pegword, "tree."

4. The next word to memorize is "cigarette." Form some mental picture that links a *cigarette* with the fourth pegword, "door."

5. The next word to memorize is "table." Form some mental picture that links a *table* with the fifth pegword, "hive."

6. The next word is "matchbook." Form some mental picture that links a *matchbook* with the sixth pegword, "sticks."

7. The next word is "glass." Form some mental picture that links a *glass* with the seventh pegword, "heaven."

8. The next word is "lamp." Form some mental picture that links a *lamp* with the eighth pegword, "gate."

9. The next word is "shoe." Form some mental picture that links a *shoe* with the ninth pegword, "line."

10. The last word is "plate." Form some mental picture that links a *plate* with the tenth pegword, "hen."

For most people, this has been an easy exercise so far. There's no difficulty in forming these mental pictures, and if your pictures were amusing in some way, then you may actually have had fun in forming them. But fun or not, this procedure has created strong memory links that will now help you in recalling the list words.

One is a bun; what was the first word you memorized? Odds are good that as soon as you think of "bun," that will call to mind the picture you formed—and that will call to mind the other word ("ashtray").

Two is a shoe; what was the second word you memorized? Three is a tree; what was the third word you memorized?

You can also take things out of order: Seven is heaven; what was the seventh word? Five is a hive; what was the fifth word? Ten is a hen; what was the tenth word?

Try to remember to test yourself again *tomorrow*. Write down the numbers 1 through 10, and try to remember the ten words you just placed in these mental pictures. If you created adequate mental pictures, you'll probably remember most of them. This provides an excellent argument that imagery can have a powerful effect on memory.

11.3   Auditory Imagery

This chapter has been about visual imagery, but imagery also exists in other modalities. For example, Ludwig van Beethoven was entirely deaf when he wrote some of his great compositions; apparently, he relied on his auditory imagery to imagine what the music would sound like. And guided by imagery, he produced extraordinary works.

Auditory imagery also gets used for more mundane purposes—including any task in which we either need to figure out what something would sound like or need to make some *judgment* about sound. For example, imagine that you saw a car with this license plate:

NE1 4 10 S

You might not get the joke until you read the symbols out loud: "Anyone for tennis?"

In the same spirit, try to figure out what familiar word or phrase is conveyed by the following sequences. But do this without making a sound. Figure these out, in other words, by *imagining* the sounds. (Answers are given on the next page.)

1. 2 6E 4 U	5. I M D 1 4 U	9. X L R 8
2. U NV ME	6. EZ 4 U 2 C	10. U4IA
3. I M A DV8	7. I M L8	11. AV8R
4. BCNU	8. I M 2 BZ	12. NML

Now, try a simple experiment. Get a friend to try this task, asking your friend to *write down* the interpretations of each of these sequences. How many does your friend get right? Now, get another friend to try the task, but *for the entire time he or she is working on the task*, ask your friend to repeat "Tah-Tah-Tah" quietly out loud. This will tie up your friend's mouth, so that he or she will not be able to "mime" the articulation of each stimulus item. How many does this friend get right? His or her performance is likely to be lower than that of your first friend, suggesting that auditory imagery often relies on the support provided by subvocalization: We imagine sounds by (silently) pronouncing them to ourselves and somehow "listening" to what we just "said."

Demonstration adapted from: Smith, D., Wilson, M., & Reisberg, D. (1996). The role of subvocalization in auditory imagery. *Neuropsychologia, 33,* 1433–1454.

Here are the answers.

1. "Too sexy for you"
2. "You envy me"
3. "I am a deviate"
4. "Be seein' you"
5. "I am the [de] one for you"
6. "Easy for you to see"
7. "I am late"
8. "I am too busy"
9. "Accelerate"
10. "Euphoria"
11. "Aviator"
12. "Animal"

Applying Cognitive Psychology

Research Methods: Expectations, Motivations, and Demand

In most experiments, we're trying to study how people behave under natural circumstances—how they behave when they're just being themselves. As a result, it is crucial that we take steps to minimize the demand character of a study.

As the textbook chapter describes, experimental *demand character* refers to any cues in the experiment that might signal to participants how they "ought to" behave. In some cases, the demand indicates to participants what results the researcher hopes for (i.e., results that would confirm the researcher's hypothesis), and this may encourage participants to make the hoped-for response, even if they're inclined toward some other option. In other cases, experimental demand character somehow suggests that certain responses are more desirable than others—so that, for example, participants perceive some responses as indicating greater intelligence or greater sensitivity. And it's plausible that participants will choose these responses to avoid appearing stupid or insensitive.

What can we do to avoid these effects, so that we don't guide participants toward some particular response but instead observe them as they normally are? Researchers use several different strategies. First, we do all we can to make sure that experimental demand character never arises in the first place. Thus, we make sure that the procedure contains no signals about what the hypothesis is or which group is receiving the experimental treatment and which group is the control. Likewise, we do what we can to phrase our questions and cast the response options that are available so that no responses seem preferable to any others.

Second, it's often a good idea to direct participants' attention *away from* the experiment's main manipulation. That way, the participants won't spend their efforts thinking about the manipulation or developing strategies in response to the manipulation. For this purpose, most experiments contain some sort of "cover story" about what the experiment is addressing. The cover story is intended to encourage participants to take the study seriously, but it is also designed to draw the participants' thinking away from the key aspects of the procedure. In this way, we decrease the risk that participants will become too cautious about, or too focused on, the main experimental manipulation, and we therefore maximize the likelihood that they'll respond naturally and spontaneously to the manipulation.

Third, we do what we can to make sure that all participants in all conditions receive exactly the same treatment. Thus, we encourage all participants in the same way, give them similar instructions, and so on. In some cases, we rely on a *double-blind procedure*, in which neither the participant nor the person administering the procedure knows what the experiment is about or which comparison group the participant is in. This ensures that the administrator won't be more encouraging or more forceful with one group in comparison with the other; it also guarantees that all participants will have the same expectations about the experiment.

Can we make certain that participants' expectations, goals, and hypotheses play *no role* in shaping our data? Probably not, and this is one of the reasons why replications (with other participants and other procedures) are so important. Even so, we do what we can to minimize the contribution of these factors, making it far more likely that our results can be understood in the terms we intend.

FOR DISCUSSION

In one of the studies discussed in the textbook chapter, participants were asked yes-or-no questions about a cat: "Does it have a head? Does it have claws? Does it have whiskers?" If participants based their answers on a mental image of a cat, their yes answers were faster for "head" than for "claws" or "whiskers," simply because the head is large and prominent in the mental picture. If, instead, participants based their answers on some other form of mental description (e.g., if they were just thinking in an abstract way about the idea of "a cat") the pattern reversed—with faster answers for "claws" and "whiskers" than for "head."

Imagine that you wanted to replicate this experiment. You would need two groups of participants: one

asked to answer your questions based on a mental picture, and one simply told to "think about cats." What would you tell the two groups, right at the start, about the purpose of the experiment or the nature of their task? Bear in mind that you wouldn't want to tell them your hypothesis; that could, by itself, create a strong experimental demand character. You also probably wouldn't tell them what *question* you're after ("I'm interested in studying how quickly people can draw information from a mental image"), because this might invite participants to generate their own hypotheses, which could somehow distort their performance. But you do need to tell them *something* to make sure they are taking your task seriously. What instructions would you give them?

Cognitive Psychology and Education: Using Imagery

Visual imagery often entertains us—in a wonderful daydream, for example, or in an exciting dream at night. But imagery is also useful in many settings. For example, the textbook chapter discusses the fact that imagery is a powerful aid to memory: We see this in the fact that materials that are easily visualized tend to be easier to remember, and also in the fact that many successful mnemonic strategies rely heavily on imagery.

However, we note one point of caution about these image-based strategies for memorizing. As the chapter makes clear, mental imagery does an excellent job of representing what something *looks like,* and so imagery mnemonics can help you a lot if you want to remember appearances—how a visualized scene looked, and what it included. To see how this might play out, imagine that you are using the mnemonic described in Demonstration 2 for this chapter, and let's say that you're working on the 10th item on the to-be-remembered list (that was the word "plate") and therefore using the tenth pegword, "hen." To remember this word, you might form a mental picture of a dinner plate underneath a delicious-looking roast chicken, with a helping of mashed potatoes alongside of it. Later, when you're trying to recall the list, you'd recite the peg-word rhyme, and so you'd be led to think, "Ten is a hen." This might call the mental picture to mind, but now what happens? Thinking about this picture, you might confidently announce, "I remember—the tenth word was 'dish'" or ". . . was 'potatoes.'" Both responses are consistent with the picture—but not with what you're trying to remember.

Likewise, in forming a mnemonic picture, you're likely to think about what the to-be-remembered items look like, and this may distract you from thinking about what these items *mean.* Imagine, for example, that you want to remember that a hypothesis was offered by the psychologist Henry Roediger. To remember this name, you might playfully convert it to "rod-digger" and form a mental picture of someone digging into the earth with a fishing rod. This will help you to remember the name, but it will encourage no insights into what Roediger's hypothesis was, or how it relates to other aspects of his theorizing, or to other things you know. Images, in other words, are excellent for remembering some things, but often what you need (or want) to remember goes beyond this.

These points are not meant to warn you against using image-based mnemonics. In fact, we've emphasized how *effective* these mnemonics are. However, it's important to understand why these mnemonics work as they do, because with that knowledge you can avoid using the mnemonics in circumstances in which the mnemonic might actually work against you.

In the same fashion, imagery can be a powerful aid to *problem-solving.* Demonstration 1 for this chapter is designed to underline this point, by making it clear how new discoveries can flow from mental pictures. But, again, there are limits on image-based problem-solving. As the textbook chapter describes, mental images are understood within a "perceptual reference frame," specifying how the imager intended the mental picture to be understood, and this frame sets powerful limits on what the imager will discover from a given mental picture.

There is, however, a way to escape these limits. People can often make new discoveries about a form by drawing a picture, based on their own mental image. The picture depicts the same form as the mental image; but because the picture is not linked to a particular reference frame, it will often support new discoveries that the original image would not. We can demonstrate this in the laboratory (e.g., in people discovering the duck in their own drawing of the duck/rabbit form, even though they failed to make the discovery from their image; see textbook, p. 357); we can also demonstrate it in real-world settings (e.g., in architects who cannot reconceptualize a building plan by scrutinizing their own mental image of the plan, but who can then make striking new discoveries once they draw out the plan on paper).

The message should be clear for anyone seeking to *use* an image as an aid to problem-solving: No matter how clear the image before the mind's eye, it is often useful to pick up a pencil and draw the image out on paper or on a blackboard; this will often facilitate new discoveries.

Once again, therefore, we see the benefits of understanding the limits of our own strategies, the limits of our own mental resources. Once you understand those limits, you can find ways to make fuller use of these strategies and resources in order to maximize your problem-solving skills, your memory, and your comprehension of new materials.

Cognitive Psychology and the Law: Lineups

There are now more than 200 cases of DNA exoneration in the United States—cases in which DNA evidence, available only after a trial was over, has shown incontrovertibly that the courts had convicted the wrong person. In each case, someone totally innocent spent years in jail, while the actually guilty person walked around free. In many cases, the innocent person, now exonerated, had been on death row awaiting execution. If the DNA evidence hadn't been available, the wrong person would have been executed.

In the vast majority of these cases, the mistaken conviction can be traced to bad eyewitness evidence: The juries had (understandably) been persuaded when an eyewitness confidently pointed to the defendant and said, "That's the man who raped me" (or "robbed me" or "shot my friend"). But in case after case, the witnesses were wrong, and the jury's decision was correspondingly mistaken.

It's crucial, therefore, to ask what we can do to avoid these incorrect identifications, and we can be guided by what we know about memory's operation in general and about memory for faces in particular. For example, research has identified a number of factors that can undermine the accuracy of an identification, and we can use these factors as a basis for deciding which identifications need to be treated with special caution. As just one illustration, we mentioned in the Cognitive Psychology and the Law essay for Chapter 3 that eyewitness identifications tend to be less accurate when the witness and the perpetrator are of different races. This suggests a need for caution when interpreting a cross-race identification, and this by itself can potentially help the courts to make better use of eyewitness evidence.

Other research has asked what steps we can take to diminish the chance of eyewitness error. For example, psychologists have offered advice on how a police lineup should be constructed—that is, what faces should be included, in addition to the suspect's—to minimize the chance of error. Evidence makes it clear that a well-chosen lineup can markedly decrease the chance of witness error, and so it is crucial, for example, that the other faces in the lineup be consistent with the witness's initial description of the perpetrator; otherwise, some lineup members may not be taken seriously as real choices for the witness, and this can guide the witness's attention to the suspect's picture, increasing the risk of a false (incorrect) identification.

We can also change the instructions given to witnesses. It is important, for example, to remind witnesses before viewing a lineup that they are under no obligation to make a choice, and that the perpetrator's face may or may not be among those presented. This instruction seems to have little effect if the perpetrator is actually present in the lineup—in essence, if he's there, you're likely to spot him. But if the perpetrator is *not* present in the lineup (i.e., if clues have led police to the wrong person), then this instruction is remarkably effective in protecting the innocent: Merely telling the witness that "the perpetrator may or may not be shown here" and "you're under no obligation to choose" seems, in some studies, to cut the risk of a false identification in half.

A different proposal concerns how the faces are shown. In a standard lineup, the witness is shown all six faces at once and must choose from among the group. In a *sequential lineup*, the witness is shown the faces one by one and must make a yes or no judgment about each one before seeing the next. This procedure has been controversial, but even so, it does seem to decrease the number of false identifications, and so may be an improvement on the standard (simultaneous) presentation.

These various points—including the procedural improvements—offer a considerable potential for improving eyewitness accuracy. It is therefore gratifying that law enforcement is taking these steps seriously with a real prospect that we can use what we know about face memory and eyewitness behavior to improve the criminal justice system.

For more on this topic

Innocence Project. (2004). http://www.innocenceproject.org

Technical Working Group on Eyewitness Evidence. (1999). *Eyewitness evidence: A guide for law enforcement*. Washington, DC: U.S. Department of Justice, Office of Justice Programs.

Wells, G. L., Malpass, R. S., Lindsay, R. C. L., Fisher, R. P., Turtle, J. W., & Fulero, S. (2000). From the lab to the police station: A successful application of eyewitness research. *American Psychologist, 55*, 581–598.

FOR DISCUSSION

On television shows, you often see the eyewitness standing behind a one-way mirror and watching as six people shuffle in and stand against a wall. The detective asks, "Is one of these men the person who robbed you?" However, this sort of *live lineup* is increasingly rare. In the United States, lineups are typically carried out with photographs—with the witness looking at six head-and-shoulder photos and trying to identify the perpetrator from this *photo lineup* (or *photomontage*). In England, lineups increasingly rely on *videos*—with the witness being shown a video of each person first looking straight ahead, then turning to the left, then turning to the right.

Think through the advantages and disadvantages of each of these three systems—live lineups, photomontages, and video lineups. Which system do you think is likely to yield the most accurate identifications? Are there considerations beyond accuracy (efficiency? speed? convenience? safety?) that might favor one of these procedures over the others?

Judgment: Drawing Conclusions From Evidence

Demonstrations

12.1 Sample Size

Research on how people make judgments suggests that our performance is at best uneven, with people in many cases drawing conclusions that are not justified by the evidence they've seen. Here, for example is a question drawn from a classic study of judgment:

> In a small town nearby, there are two hospitals. Hospital A has an average of 45 births per day; Hospital B is smaller and has an average of 15 births per day. As we all know, overall the proportion of males born is 50%. Each hospital recorded the number of days in which, on that day, at least 60% of the babies born were male.
>   Which hospital recorded more such days?
>   a. Hospital A
>   b. Hospital B
>   c. both equal

What's your answer to this question? In more formal procedures, the majority of research participants choose response (c), "both equal," but this answer is statistically unwarranted. All of the births in the country add up to a 50-50 split between male and female babies. The larger the sample one examines, the more likely one is to approximate this ideal. Conversely, the smaller the sample one examines, the more likely one is to stray from this ideal. Days with 60% male births, straying from the ideal, are therefore more likely in the smaller hospital, Hospital B.

If you don't see this, consider a more extreme case:

Hospital C has 1,000 births per day; Hospital D has exactly 1 birth per day. Which hospital records more days with at least 90% male births?

This value will be observed in Hospital D rather often, since on many days all the babies born (one out of one) will be male. This value is surely less likely, though, in Hospital C: 900 male births, with just 100 female, would be a remarkable event indeed. In this case, it seems clear that the smaller hospital can more easily stray far from the 50-50 split.

In the hospital problem, participants seem not to take sample size into account. They seem to think a particular pattern is just as likely with a small sample as with a large sample, although this is plainly not true. This belief, however, is just what one would expect if people were relying on the *representativeness heuristic*, making the assumption that each instance of a category—or, in this case, each subset of a larger set—should show the properties associated with the entire set.

Try this question with a couple of your friends. As you'll see, it's extraordinarily easy to find people who choose the incorrect option ("both equal"), underlining just how often people seem to be insensitive to considerations of sample size.

Demonstration adapted from: Kahneman, D., & Tversky, A. (1972). Subjective probability: A judgment of representativeness. *Cognitive Psychology, 3,* 430–454.

12.2   Relying on the Representative Heuristic

Demonstration 1 indicated that some people often neglect (or misunderstand the meaning of) *sample size*. In other cases, some people's judgment relies on heuristics that are not in any way guided by *logic*, and so their conclusion ends up being quite illogical. For example, here is another classic problem from research on judgment:

Linda is 31 years old, single, outspoken, and very bright. She majored in philosophy. As a student, she was deeply concerned with issues of discrimination and social justice, and she also participated in anti-nuclear demonstrations.
  Which of the following is more likely to be true?
  a. Linda is a bank teller.
  b. Linda is a bank teller and is active in the feminist movement.

What's your response? In many studies, a clear majority of participants (sometimes as high as 85%) choose option (b). Logically, though, this makes no sense. If Linda is a feminist bank teller, then she is still a bank teller. Therefore, there's no way for option

(b) to be true without option (a) also being true. Therefore, option (b) couldn't possibly be more likely than option (a)! Choosing option (b), in other words, is akin to saying that if we randomly choose someone who lives in North America, the chance of that person being from Vermont is greater than the chance of that person being from the United States.

Why, therefore, do so many people choose option (b)? This option makes sense if people are relying on the representativeness heuristic. In that case, they make the category judgment by asking themselves: "How much does Linda resemble my idea of a bank teller? How much does she resemble my idea of a *feminist* bank teller?" On this basis, they could easily be led to option (b), because the description of Linda does, in fact, encourage a particular view of her and her politics.

There is, however, another possibility. With options (a) and (b) sitting side-by-side, someone might say: "Well, if option (b) is talking about the bank teller who *is* a feminist, then option (a) must be talking about a bank teller who is *not* a feminist." On that interpretation, choosing option (b) does seem reasonable. Is this how you interpreted option (a)?

You might spend a moment thinking about how to test this alternative interpretation—the idea that research participants interpret option (a) in this narrowed fashion. One strategy is to present option (a) to some participants and ask them how likely it is, and to present option (b) *to other participants* and ask them how likely it is. In this way, there's no comparison between options, and so no implied contrast in the options. In this situation, there's no reason at all for participants to interpret option (a) in the narrowed fashion. Even so, in studies using this alternative procedure, the group of participants seeing option (a) still rated it as *less likely* than the other group of participants rated the option they saw. Again, this makes no sense from the standpoint of logic, but it makes perfect sense if participants are using the representativeness heuristic.

Demonstration adapted from: Tversky, A., & Kahneman, D. (1983). Extension versus intuitive reasoning: The conjunction fallacy in probability judgment. *Psychological Review, 90*, 293–315.

12.3   Applying Base Rates

Chapter 12 documents many errors in judgment, and it is especially troubling that these errors can be found even when highly knowledgable and experienced experts are making judgments about domains that are enormously consequential. As an illustration, consider the following scenario.

Imagine that someone you care about—let's call her Julia, age 42—is worried that she might have breast cancer. In thinking about Julia's case, we might start by asking: How common is breast cancer for women of Julia's age, with her family history, her dietary pattern, and so on? Let us assume that for this group the statistics show an overall 3% likelihood of developing breast cancer. This should be reassuring to Julia, because there is a 97% chance that she is cancer free.

Of course, a 3% chance is still enormously scary for this disease, and so Julia decides to get a mammogram. When her results come back, the report is bad—indicating that she does have breast cancer. Julia quickly does some research to find out how accurate mammograms are, and she learns that the available data are something like this:

	Mammogram indicates	
	Cancer	No cancer
Cancer actually present	85%	15%
Cancer actually absent	10%	90%

In light of all this information, what is your best estimate of the chance that Julia does, in fact, have breast cancer? She's gotten a bad mammogram result, and the test seems, according to her research, accurate. What should we conclude? *Think about this for a few moments, and estimate the percentage chance of Julia having breast cancer before reading on.*

When medical doctors are asked questions like these, their answers are often wildly inaccurate because they (like most people) fail to use base-rate information correctly. What was your estimate of the percentage chance of Julia having breast cancer? The correct answer is 20%. This is an awful number, given what's at stake, and Julia would surely want to pursue further tests. But the odds are still heavily in Julia's favor, with a 4-to-1 chance that she is *entirely free of cancer.*

Where does this answer come from? Let's fill in the table below, but using *actual counts* rather than the percentages shown in the previous table. Imagine that we are considering 100,000 women with medical backgrounds similar to Julia's. We have already said that overall there is a 3% chance of breast cancer in this group, and so 3,000 (3% of 100,000) of these women will have breast cancer. Let's fill that number in as the *top* number in the "Total number" column, and this will leave the rest of the overall group (97,000) as the *bottom* number in this column.

	Mammogram indicates		
	Cancer	No cancer	Total number
Cancer actually present			3,000
Cancer actually absent			97,000

Now, let's fill in the rows. There are 3,000 women counted in the top row, and we've already said that in this group the mammogram will (correctly) indicate that cancer is present in 85% of the cases. So the number for "Mammogram indicates cancer" in the top row will be 85% of the total in this row (3,000), or 2,550. The number of cases for "Mammogram indicates no cancer" in this row will be the remaining 15% of the 3,000, so fill in that number—450.

Do the same for the bottom row. We've already said that there are 97,000 women represented in this row; of these, the mammogram will correctly indicate *no* cancer for 90% (87,300) and will falsely indicate cancer for 10% (9,700). Fill those numbers in the appropriate positions.

Now, let's put these pieces together. According to our numbers, a total of 12,250 will receive the horrid information that they have breast cancer. (That's the total number of the two cells in the left column, "Mammogram indicates cancer.") Within this group, this test result will be correct for 2,550 women (left column, top row). The result will be misleading for the remaining 9,700 (left column, bottom row). Thus, *of the women receiving awful news from their mammogram, 2,550 ÷ 12,250, or 20%, will actually have breast cancer; the remaining 80% will be cancer free.*

Notice, then, that the mammogram is *wrong* far more often than it's right. This is not because the mammogram is an inaccurate test. In fact, the test is rather accurate. However, if the test is used with patient groups for which the base rate is low, then the mammogram might be wrong in only 10% of the cancer-free cases, but this will be 10% of a large number, producing a substantial number of horrifying false alarms.

This is obviously a consequential example, because we are discussing a disease that is lethal in many cases. It is therefore deeply troubling that even in this very important example, people still make errors of judgment. Worse, it's striking that experienced physicians, when asked the same questions, also make errors—they, too, ignore the base rates and therefore give risk estimates that are off by a very wide margin.

At the same time, because this is a consequential example, let's add some caution to these points. First, if a woman has a different background from Julia (our hypothetical patient), then her overall risk for breast cancer may be higher than Julia's. In other words, the base rate for her group may be higher or lower (depending on the woman's age, exposure to certain toxins, family history, and other factors), and this will have a huge impact on the calculations we have discussed here. Therefore, we cannot freely generalize from the numbers considered here to other cases; we would need to know the base rate for these other cases.

Second, even if Julia's risk is 20%, this is still a very high number, and so Julia (or anyone in this situation) would obviously want to pursue further testing and, possibly, treatment for this life-threatening illness. A 1-in-5 chance of having a deadly disease must be taken very seriously! However, this does not change the fact that a 20% risk is very different from the 85% risk that one might fear if one considered only the mammogram results in isolation from the base rates. At 20%, the odds are good that Julia is safe; at 85%, she almost certainly has this disease. It seems likely that this is a difference that would matter for Julia's subsequent steps, and it reminds us that medical decision-making needs to be guided by full information—including, it seems, information about base rates.

Demonstration adapted from: Eddy, D. (1982). Probabilistic reasoning in clinical medicine. In D. Kahneman, P. Slovic, & A. Tversky (Eds.), *Judgment under uncertainty: Heuristics and biases* (pp. 249–267). Cambridge, England: Cambridge University Press.

Applying Cognitive Psychology

Research Methods: Systematic Data Collection

In our daily lives, we frequently rely on judgment and reasoning *heuristics*—shortcuts that usually lead to the correct conclusion but that sometimes produce error. As a direct result, we sometimes draw inappropriate conclusions, but these errors are simply the price we pay for the heuristics' efficiency. To avoid the errors, we'd need to employ reasoning strategies that would require much more time and effort than the heuristics do.

For scientists, though, efficiency is less of a priority; it's okay if we need months or even years to test a hypothesis. And, of course, accuracy is crucial for scientists: We want to make certain our claims are correct and our conclusions fully warranted. For these reasons, scientists need to step away from the reasoning strategies we all use in our day-to-day lives and to rely instead on more laborious, but more accurate, forms of reasoning.

How exactly does scientific reasoning differ from ordinary day-to-day reasoning? The answer has many parts, but one part is directly relevant to points prominent in Chapter 12 of the textbook: In ordinary reasoning, people are heavily influenced by whatever data are easily available to them—the observations that they can think of first, when they consider an issue; or the experiences that happen to be prominent in their memory, when they try to think of cases pertinent to some question. Of course, this is a risky way to proceed, because the evidence that's easily available to someone may not be representative of the broader patterns in the world. Why is this? Some evidence is more available to us because it's easier to remember than other (perhaps more common) observations. Some evidence is more available to us because it's been showcased by the media. And some evidence is more available to us because of the pattern known as *confirmation bias*. This term refers to the fact that when people search for evidence they often look only for evidence that might *support* their views; they do little to collect evidence that might challenge those views. This can lead to a lopsided view of the facts—and an inaccurate judgment.

To avoid these problems, scientists insist on systematic data collection. This rules out arguments based on *anecdotal evidence*—evidence that has been informally collected and reported—because an anecdote may represent a highly atypical case or may provide only one person's description of the data, with no way for us to find out if that description is accurate or not. We also have no way of knowing how the anecdote was selected—with a real possibility that thanks to confirmation bias, the anecdote is being offered merely because it fits with the beliefs of the person reporting the anecdote.

Overall, therefore, scientists need to collect the data in a fashion that accurately and objectively records the facts, and they also need to collect *enough* evidence so that they're not persuaded by a couple of salient cases (what the Chapter 12 text identifies as "man who" stories). They also must set up their data collection in a fashion that guarantees equal emphasis on the facts that support their hypothesis and the facts that do not.

These points have many implications, including implications for how we choose our participants (we can't just gather data from people likely to support our views) and also for how we design our procedures. The requirement of systematic data collection also shapes how the data will be recorded. For example, we cannot rely on our memory for the data, because it's possible that we might remember just those cases that fit with our interpretation. Likewise, we cannot treat the facts we like differently from the facts we don't like, so that, perhaps, we're more alert to flaws in the observations that conflict with our hypotheses or less likely to report these observations to others.

Scientists also take steps to combat another form of confirmation bias—the *file-drawer problem.* This term refers to the fact that investigators might choose not to publish disappointing results (i.e., results that don't confirm their hypothesis); instead, the data are—so to speak—dumped into a file drawer and potentially forgotten. As one example, many studies have looked for differences in intellectual performance between men and women. In the majority of studies the data show no difference, suggesting that intellectually men and women are quite similar. However, this *null finding* (a finding of "no difference") is not impressive to many people, and so these results never get published. When an occasional study does find a sex difference, though, this is intriguing, and so it does get published (and maybe even reported in the mainstream media). As a result, the data that are "visible" to us all are biased—representing one side of the story but not the other.

Scientists rely on several precautions to guard against the file-drawer problem. The most obvious safeguard is the requirement that scientists periodically gather together all of the evidence on an issue, including unpublished results. This full data pattern is then reported in a *review article* that considers all of the findings, not just those on one side of an issue.

Clearly, then, many elements are involved in systematic data collection. But all of these elements are crucial if we are to make certain our hypotheses have been fully and fairly tested. In this regard, scientific conclusions are invariably on a firmer footing than the judgments we offer as part of our daily experience.

FOR DISCUSSION

Imagine that a friend of yours comments: "You know, strange things influence human behavior. For example, in most cities, the crime rate goes up whenever the moon is full. Why do you think that is?" You might, in conversation, try to answer your friend's question and seek explanations for this curious phenomenon. Before you do, though, you might ask a question of your own: "Are we sure we've got the facts right? Is it really true that crimes are more common at certain phases of the moon?"

If you really wanted to check on this claim—that crime rates are linked to the moon's phase—what systematic data would you need? How would you collect and record the data, making certain to avoid the problems discussed in this essay?

Cognitive Psychology and Education:
Making People Smarter

In some ways, Chapter 12 of the textbook offers some scary claims: People often make errors in judgment. These errors occur even when people are motivated to be careful and trying to be accurate in their conclusions. The errors occur even when people are making consequential—and perhaps even life-changing—judgments. The errors also occur even among practiced professionals, including therapists thinking about psychological diagnoses, and physicians thinking about medical diagnoses.

But the chapter also offers some encouragement: We can take certain steps that improve people's judgments. Some of those steps involve changes in the environment. We can, for example, ensure that the evidence we consider, or the evidence we present to others, has been converted to *frequencies* (e.g., "4 cases out of 100") rather than percentages ("4%") or proportions (".04"); this, it seems, is enough on its own to make our judgments more accurate and to increase the likelihood that we'll consider base rates when drawing our conclusions.

Other steps, in contrast, involve *education*. As the chapter mentions, training students in *statistics* seems to improve their ability to think about evidence—including evidence that is obviously quantitative (e.g., a baseball player's batting average or someone's exam scores) and evidence that is not, at first appearance, quantitative (e.g., thinking about how you should interpret a dancer's audition or someone's job interview). The benefits of statistics training are great—with some studies showing error rates in subsequent reasoning essentially cut in half.

The key element in statistical training is probably not in the mathematics per se. It is valuable, for a number of purposes, to know the derivation of statistical equations or to know exactly how to use certain statistics software packages. For the improvement of everyday judgment, however, the key involves the new perspective that a statistics course encourages: This perspective helps you to realize that certain observations (e.g., an audition or an interview) can be thought of as a *sample* of evidence, drawn from a larger pool of observations that potentially one could have made. The perspective also alerts you to the fact that a sample may not be representative of a broader population and that larger samples are more likely to be representative. For purposes of the statistics course itself, these are relatively simple points; but being alert to these points can have striking and widespread consequences in your thinking about issues entirely separate from the topics and examples covered in the statistics class.

In fact, once we cast things in this way, it becomes clear that other forms of education can also have the same benefit. Many courses in psychology, for example, or sociology, or political science, will also include coverage of methodological issues. These courses can also highlight the fact that a single observation is just a sample and that a small sample sometimes cannot be trusted. These courses sometimes cover topics that might reveal (and warn you against) confirmation bias or caution against the dangers of informally collected evidence. On this basis, it seems likely that other courses (and not just statistics classes) can actually improve your everyday thinking—and, in fact, several studies strongly confirm this optimistic conclusion.

A college education cannot, by itself, turn you into a flawless thinker who never makes judgment errors. Indeed, perhaps nothing could turn people into flawless thinkers. But there is reason to believe that many courses that you take can improve your day-to-day thinking. The best courses are likely to be those that focus on the interpretation of evidence—if possible, quantitative evidence—so that you are forced to think about issues of sampling and variability. It will also be best if the courses focus on somewhat *messy* evidence, so that you are forced to confront the difficulties of dealing with ambiguous or uncertain results—just as you must in daily life.

For more on this topic

Fong, G., & Nisbett, R. (1991). Immediate and delayed transfer of training effects in statistical reasoning. *Journal of Experimental Psychology: General, 120,* 34–45.

Lehman, D. R., Lempert, R. O., & Nisbett, R. E. (1988). The effects of graduate training on reasoning: Formal discipline and thinking about everyday-life events. *American Psychologist, 43*(6), 431–442.

Lehman, D., & Nisbett, R. (1990). A longitudinal study of the effects of undergraduate training on reasoning. *Developmental Psychology, 26,* 952–960.

Cognitive Psychology and the Law: Juries' Judgment

Our focus in Chapter 12 of the textbook was on how people draw conclusions based on the evidence they encounter. Of course, this is exactly what a judge or jury needs to do in a trial—reach a conclusion (a verdict) based on the trial evidence. Can we therefore use what we know about judgment in other contexts to illuminate how judges and juries perform their task?

Consider, as one example, the separation between System 1 and System 2 thinking: System 1 thinking, we've argued in the textbook chapter, is fast and automatic, but it can sometimes lead to error. System 2 thinking, in contrast, is slower and more effortful, but it can often catch those errors, leading to better judgment. The problem, though, is that people often rely on System 1 even for deeply consequential judgments. System 2, it seems, enters the scene only if appropriately triggered.

How does this play out in the courts? Consider, as one crucial case, the problem of racial prejudice in the legal system. It turns out that Blacks are more likely to be convicted than Whites are, even if we focus our attention on cases in which the crimes themselves are the same in the comparison between the races, and if the evidence and circumstances are quite similar. Then, when convicted, Blacks are likely to receive more severe punishments than Whites—including the death penalty.

What produces these race differences? One troubling hypothesis is that many people involved in the criminal justice system—including police, judges, and juries—are influenced by an easy and automatic association, provided by System 1 thinking, that links Blacks to thoughts of crime. This association may not reflect a belief, in the person's mind, that Blacks are often guilty of crimes. Instead, the association may indicate only that the ideas of "Blacks" and "crime" are somehow linked in memory (perhaps because of images in the media or some other external influence). As a result of this linkage, activating one of the ideas can trigger the other, and this association may be enough to shape a System 1 judgment. This is because, after all, System 1 typically relies on the ideas that come effortlessly to mind; and so, if the idea of "Blacks" triggers the idea of "crime," this can lead to a prejudiced conclusion.

Can we use System 2 to override this effect? In a number of studies, researchers have simply called participants' attention to the fact that a particular trial defendant is, in fact, a Black and that considerations of race may be pertinent to the case. Surprisingly, this is sometimes enough to put participants on their guard, so that they resist the easy conclusion that might be suggested by memory associations. As a result, merely making race explicit as a trial issue can sometimes diminish juror prejudice.

However, this surely does not mean that in general we can erase the effects of prejudice merely by calling jurors' attention to the defendant's race; the situation is more complicated than this. In some cases, in fact, alerting jurors to the issue of race may *increase* prejudice rather than diminish it. (This would be true if, for example, the jurors were overtly racist, or if the jurors were convinced that the *police* were racist. In the latter case, thinking about the trial in racial terms might unfairly bias the jury in favor of the defendant.) There is, in other words, likely to be no simple step we can take to guarantee courtroom procedures that are free of bias.

Even so, the research provides us with one clue about how we might improve the system, and at the same time it reminds us that we do need to consider how courtroom judgments can be shaped by System 1 thinking. What steps we can take to deal with this (and how, for example, we can ensure that System 1's prejudices are overruled by the more careful thinking of System 2) is an urgent matter for future research.

For more on this topic

Correll, J., Park, B., Judd, C. M., & Wittenbrink, B. (2002). The police officer's dilemma: Using ethnicity to disambiguate potentially threatening individuals. *Journal of Personality and Social Psychology, 83,* 1314–1329.

Dovidio, J. F., Kawakami, K., & Gaertner, S. L. (2002). Implicit and explicit prejudice and interracial interaction. *Journal of Personality and Social Psychology, 82,* 62–68.

Sommers, S. R., & Ellsworth, P. C. (2001). White juror bias: An investigation of prejudice against black defendants in the American courtroom. *Psychology, Public Policy, and Law, 7,* 201–229.

FOR DISCUSSION

Some people would argue that the distinction between System 1 and System 2 is *irrelevant* for the legal system. They would suggest that judges and juries know they are making enormously important decisions, and this would, by itself, be enough to motivate judges and juries to use the more careful, more accurate System 2. For judgments as important as a courtroom verdict, it would be irresponsible to rely on System 1's "shortcuts." Likewise, some people would suggest that judges are experienced and skilled in thinking about courtroom issues; this should virtually guarantee that judges would "rise above" the shortcuts inherent in System 1 and rely instead on the more accurate processes of System 2.

Unfortunately, though, the textbook chapter provides indications that these arguments are wrong and that System 1 is likely to play a role in the courts—no matter how consequential the issues or how experienced the judges. What is the evidence, within the chapter, that might be relevant to these crucial points?

CHAPTER 13

Reasoning: Thinking Through the Implications of What You Know

Demonstrations

13.1 Framing Questions

What are the factors that influence our decisions? What are the factors that *should* influence our decisions? Evidence suggests that the "frame" of a decision plays an important role; should it?

Recruit four friends for this demonstration. Ask two of them this question:

> Imagine that you are part of a team, working for a medium-sized company, trying to decide how to invest $10,000,000. You have just learned about a new stock-market fund that has, in the last 5 years, outperformed 75% of its competitors.
>   What percentage of the $10,000,000 would you want to invest in this stock-market fund?

Ask two other friends this question:

> Imagine that you are part of a team, working for a medium-sized company, trying to decide how to invest $10,000,000. You have just learned about a new stock-market fund that has, in the last 5 years, been outperformed by 25% of its competitors.
>   What percentage of the $10,000,000 would you want to invest in this stock-market fund?

According to a straightforward economic analysis, these two versions of this question should yield identical information—outperforming 75% of a group is the same as being outperformed by 25% of the group. According to the points in the textbook chapter, though, this difference in frame may change how people react to the questions. Can you predict which group will be more likely to invest heavily in the fund?

The chapter mentions that in general the framing of a question guides what people pay attention to in their decision-making and how they assess their options. We know, for example, that physicians are more likely to recommend a new medication if they've been told that the treatment has a 50% success rate, rather than being told that it has a 50% failure rate. People are more likely to buy ground meat that is 90% fat-free rather than meat that is 10% fat. It seems likely, therefore, that your friends will be more likely to invest heavily in the fund in the first frame described here, rather than the second.

Demonstration adapted from: Tversky, A., & Kahneman, D. (1981). The framing of decisions and the psychology of choice. *Science, 211,* 453–458.

13.2   The Effect of Content on Reasoning

In the textbook chapter, we note that *how people reason* is heavily influenced by the *content* of what they are reasoning about, and this is not what we would expect if people were using the rules of logic. This can be demonstrated through a variation on the four-card task discussed in Chapter 13.

Imagine that you are the *owner* of a large company. You are concerned that your employees have been taking days off even when they are not entitled to do so. The company's rule is:

> If an employee works on the weekend, then that person gets a day off during the week.

Here are employment records for four employees. Each record indicates, on one side, whether the employee has worked on the weekend or not. The record indicates, on the other side, whether that person got a day off or not.

As the owner of this business, which records would you want to inspect to make sure that your rule is being followed? Place an *X* under the cards that you would turn over.

Now, imagine that you are a *worker* in the same large company. You are concerned that your boss is not giving people their days off, even when they have earned the days off.

Which records would you want to inspect to make sure that the company's rule is being followed? Place an *X* under the cards that you would turn over.

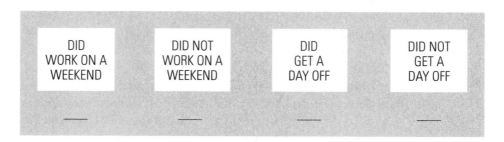

Most people give different answers to these two questions. As a *company owner*, they turn over the middle two cards—to make sure that the person who didn't work on a weekend isn't taking an "illegal" day off, and to make sure the person who did take a day off really earned it. As a *worker*, they tend to turn over the first and last cards—to make sure that everyone who earned a day off gets one.

In the textbook chapter, we discuss three different theories that can be applied to understanding why performance on any four-card problem depends on the problem's content. One theory was cast in terms of evolution, with an emphasis on how people reason when they're thinking about "cheaters." A second theory was cast in terms of pragmatic reasoning, on the idea that people have learned, during their lifetime, how to think about situations involving *permission* and situations involving *obligation*. A third theory suggested that people use a problem's content to figure out if the "if clause" (the condition) identifies a *necessary condition* or a *sufficient condition*. Which of these theories fit with the fact that selections in the four-card problem presented above change if your perspective changes (e.g., from the owner's perspective to the worker's perspective)? In fact, all three theories fit with this result; do you see how?

Demonstration adapted from: Gigerenzer, G., & Hug, K. (1992). Domain-specific reasoning: Social contracts, cheating and perspective change. *Cognition, 43,* 127–171.

13.3   Mental Accounting

In the textbook chapter, we consider evidence that people seek reasons when making a decision, and they select an option only when they see a good reason to make that choice. But *how* do people seek reasons, and what reasons do they find persuasive? We can get some insights on this problem by looking at various decisions that people make. For example, imagine that you are at an electronics store and about to purchase a pair of headphones for $145 and a calculator for $20. Your friend mentions, though, that the same calculator is on sale for $10 at a different store located 20 minutes away.

Would you make the trip to the other store? Think about it for a moment. Poll a few friends to find out if they decide the same way.

Now, imagine a different scenario. You are at an electronics store and about to purchase a pair of headphones for $20 and a calculator for $145. Your friend mentions that the same calculator is on sale for $135 at a different store located 20 minutes away.

In this case, would you make the trip to the other store? Think about it and decide, and again poll a few friends.

Most people *would* go to the other store in the first scenario, but they *would not* go in the second scenario. Of course, in either of these scenarios, your total purchase will be $165 if you buy both items at the first store, and $155 if you buy both items at the second store. In both cases, therefore, the decision depends on whether you think a savings of $10 is enough to justify a 20-minute trip. Even so, people react to the two problems differently, as if they were dividing their purchases into different "accounts." If the $10 savings comes from the smaller account, then it seems like a great deal (the calculator is 50% cheaper!). If the savings comes from the more expensive account, it seems much less persuasive (less than 7%).

It seems clear, then, that our theories of decision-making must include principles of "mental accounting," principles that will describe how we separate our gains and losses, our income and our expenses, into separate "budget categories." These principles are likely to be complex, and it's not obvious why, in our example, people seem to regard the calculator and the headphone purchases as separate (rather than, say, just thinking about them under the broader label "supplies"). But the fact is that people do think of these purchases as separate, and this influences their decision-making. Therefore, complicated or not, principles of mental accounting must become part of our overall theorizing.

Demonstration adapted from: Thaler, R. (1999). Mental accounting matters. *Journal of Behavioral Decision Making, 12,* 183–206.

Applying Cognitive Psychology

Research Methods: The Community of Scientists

We have discussed many of the steps that scientists take to ensure that their data are persuasive and their claims are correct. We need to add to our discussion, though, another important factor that keeps scientific claims on track—namely, the fact that scientists do not work in isolation from each other. To see how this matters, consider the phenomenon of *confirmation bias*, discussed in both Chapters 12 and 13 in the textbook. This broad term refers to a number of different effects, all of which have the result of protecting our beliefs from serious challenge. Thus, for example, when we're evaluating our beliefs, we tend to seek out information that might confirm our beliefs rather than information that might undermine them. Likewise, if we encounter information that is at all ambiguous, we are likely to interpret the information in a fashion that brings it into line with our beliefs. And so on.

Scientists do what they can to avoid this bias, but even so, scientists are, in the end, vulnerable to the same problems as everyone else, and so it's no surprise that confirmation bias can be detected in scientific reasoning. Thus, when scientists encounter facts that fit with their preferred hypothesis, they tend to accept those facts as they are; when they encounter facts that don't fit, they scrutinize the facts with special care, seeking problems or flaws.

Some scholars, however, have argued that confirmation bias can sometimes be a *good thing* for scientists. After all, it takes enormous effort to develop, test, and defend a scientific theory and, eventually, to persuade others to take that theory seriously. All of this effort requires considerable motivation and commitment from the theory's advocates, and confirmation bias may help them to maintain this commitment. This helps us understand why, according to several studies, the scientists most guilty of confirmation bias are often those who are considered most important and influential by their peers.

These points, however, do not diminish the serious problems that confirmation bias can create. How, therefore, do scientists manage to gain the advantages (in motivation) that confirmation bias creates, without suffering the negative consequences of this bias? The answer lies in the fact that science depends on the activity of a *community* of scientists. Within this community, each scientist has his or her own views, and so the confirmation bias of one researcher, favoring one hypothesis, is likely to be counteracted by the confirmation bias of some other researcher who prefers an alternate hypothesis. As a result, each scientist will subject the others' evidence to special scrutiny, so that in the end all data are scrutinized—just as we want.

To promote this scrutiny, scientists rely on a *peer-review process*. Before a new finding or new claim is taken seriously, it must be published in a scientific journal. (Linked to this, the scientific community is very wary when a research team decides to jump ahead and announce a new result in a news conference before the result has been properly published.) And before any article can be published, it must be evaluated by the journal's editor (usually, a scientist with impressive credentials) and three or four experts in the field. (These are the "peers" who "review" the paper.) The reviewers are chosen by the editor to represent a variety of perspectives—including, if possible, a perspective likely to be critical of the paper's claims. If these reviewers find problems in the method or the interpretation of the results, the article will not be published by the journal. Thus, any article that appears in print must have survived this careful evaluation—an essential form of quality control.

In addition, publication itself is also important. At the least, publication makes the finding accessible to the broader community and therefore open to scrutiny, criticism, and—if appropriate—attack. In addition, once the details of a study are available in print, other scientists can try to reproduce the experiment to make sure that the result is reliable. (For more on the importance of such *replication*, see the Research Methods for Chapter 5.) These are significant long-term benefits from publication.

In short, we should take a hypothesis seriously only after it has received the careful scrutiny of many scientists, reviewing the hypothesis from a variety of perspectives. This ensures that the hypothesis has been examined both by scientists inclined to protect the hypothesis and by others inclined to reject it, guaranteeing that the hypothesis has been carefully, fully, and persuasively tested. In this fashion the scientific community gains from the commitment and motivation that are the good sides of confirmation bias, without suffering the problems associated with this bias.

For more on this topic

Tweney, R., Dyharty, M., & Mynatt, C. (1981). *On scientific thinking.* New York: Columbia University Press.

FOR DISCUSSION

As this essay describes, confirmation bias is not always a bad thing. A strong commitment to your own beliefs, to your own ideas, can provide you with the motivation you need to pursue your beliefs—testing them, refining them, presenting them to others. Without this commitment, you might end up being too tentative and not at all persuasive when you present your beliefs.

It would seem, then, that what we really need is a balance—a commitment to pursuing and developing our own beliefs, but also a willingness, in the end, to admit that we are wrong if that's what the evidence tells us. But how should we define that balance? The answer depends on several factors. Imagine, as one example, that you're standing in the supermarket and see a tabloid headline: "Herd of Unicorns Located on Tropical Island." Would you abandon your belief that there are no unicorns? Or would you give in to confirmation bias and overrule this evidence? Imagine, likewise, that a high school physics stu-

dent, in a lab exercise, finds evidence contradicting the Newtonian claim that $F = ma$. Would you abandon your belief that Newton was correct? Or would you give in to confirmation bias and overrule this evidence, too?

Based on these examples, can you develop some ideas or principles that might guide us in thinking about when confirmation bias is more acceptable and when it is less so? Why is it that in these examples you probably gave in to confirmation bias and were not inclined to give up your current ideas? (As a hint: Should confirmation bias be stronger when the challenge to your belief comes from a source of uncertain quality? Should confirmation bias be stronger when the belief being tested is already well supported by other evidence? Should confirmation bias be stronger when you're first trying to develop an idea, so that perhaps the idea isn't ready for testing? Thinking through these points will help you figure out when confirmation bias is a real problem and when it's not.)

Cognitive Psychology and Education:
Choosing Your Courses

Most universities have some sort of collegewide graduation requirements. Students are often required to take a certain number of courses in mathematics, or perhaps a foreign language. They are often required to take courses in the humanities or in laboratory science.

How should we think about these requirements? One widely endorsed view is the *doctrine of formal disciplines.* The idea, roughly, is that our reasoning and judgment rely on certain formal rules—akin to the rules of logic or mathematics—and so we'll think best (most clearly, more rationally) if we are well practiced in using these rules. Therefore, education should emphasize the academic disciplines that rely on these formal rules: math; logic; and, according to some people, linguistics and the study of languages. (This is presumably because the study of languages sensitizes students to the formal properties of language.)

Chapter 13, however, challenges this doctrine. There are, to be sure, excellent reasons why you should take courses in math, logic, and language. But it's a mistake to argue that these disciplines somehow strengthen the mind in a fashion that improves thinking in general. Why is this? First, the chapter makes it clear that reasoning and judgment do not rely on formal rules (i.e., rules, like those of math or logic, that depend only on the *form* of the argument being considered). Instead, reasoning and judgment depend heavily on the *content* that we're thinking about. It's therefore wrong to claim that formal disciplines give us training and exercise in the rules we use all the time; we do not, in fact, use these rules all the time.

Second, a number of studies have asked directly whether training in logic, or training in abstract mathematics, improves reasoning in everyday affairs. They do not. We mentioned in Chapter 12 that training in *statistics* improves judgment, but the key aspect of this training is likely to be the exercise in "translating" everyday cases into statistical terms, and not knowing the mathematical formulations themselves. Likewise, some studies do suggest that the study of languages is associated with improved academic performance, but these studies are potentially misleading. Specifically, it is true that students who take Latin in high school do better on the Scholastic Aptitude Test and often do better in college. But this is probably not because taking Latin helped these students; instead, it is probably because the students who choose to take Latin are likely to be more ambitious, more academically motivated, in the first place.

How, therefore, should we design students' education? What courses should the university recommend, and what courses should you seek out if you want to improve your critical thinking skills? Part of the answer was offered in Chapter 12's Cognitive Psychology and Education essay: Your ability to make judgments does seem to be improved by courses in statistics and courses in the academic disciplines that rely on quantitative *but somewhat messy* data—disciplines such as psychology, sociology, courses at the quantitative end of anthropology, and so on. And part of the answer is suggested by Chapter 13: We mentioned there that people often seem to rely on pragmatic, goal-oriented rules—rules involving permission or obligation, rules tied to the pragmatic ways we try to figure out cause-and-effect relationships ("If this broken switch is causing the problem, my car will work once I replace the switch").

One might think, therefore, that reasoning will be improved by practice in thinking in these pragmatic terms—and evidence suggests that this is right. Short episodes of training, reminding people of the procedures needed for thinking about permission or encouraging people to think through different cause-and-effect relationships, do seem to improve reasoning. Likewise, *professional* training of the right sort also helps. Lawyers, for example, get lots of practice in thinking about *permission* and *obligation;* studies suggest that this training helps lawyers to think through a variety of pragmatic, day-to-day problems that have little to do with their legal practice.

Notice, then, that there are two messages here. The broad message is that we can use our scientific studies of how people *do* think to start generating hypotheses about how we can *train* people to think more effectively. Then, at a more specific level, we can start making some recommendations: Again, training in math or logic is valuable, but not because it will make you a better thinker. For purposes of sharpening your everyday thinking skills, courses that involve detailed analysis of cause-and-effect, and courses that involve thinking about obligations and permissions, may be the way to go.

For more on this topic

Fong, G., & Nisbett, R. (1991). Immediate and delayed transfer of training effects in statistical reasoning. *Journal of Experimental Psychology: General, 120,* 34–45.

Lehman, D. R., Lempert, R. O., & Nisbett, R. E. (1988). The effects of graduate training on reasoning: Formal discipline and thinking about everyday-life events. *American Psychologist, 43*(6), 431–442.

Lehman, D., & Nisbett, R. (1990). A longitudinal study of the effects of undergraduate training on reasoning. *Developmental Psychology, 26,* 952–960.

Cognitive Psychology and the Law: Judgment Biases in the Courtroom

As Chapter 13 describes, reasoning can be pulled off track by many factors, so that our conclusions are sometimes less logical, less justified, than we would wish. How does this apply to the courts?

In many trials, potential jurors are exposed to media coverage of the crime prior to the trial's start, and this pretrial publicity can have many effects. One concern is the pattern called *belief bias.* In the lab, this term refers to a tendency to consider an argument "more logical" if it leads to a conclusion that the person believed to begin with. In the courtroom, this could translate into a juror's evaluating the trial arguments not on their own terms, but in terms of whether the arguments led to the conclusion the juror would have endorsed (based on the media coverage) at the trial's start. This influence of information from outside the courthouse is contrary to the rules of a trial, but jurors may be unable to resist this powerful effect.

As a related concern, consider the effect called *confirmation bias.* As the textbook chapter discusses, this bias takes many forms, including a tendency to accept evidence favoring one's own views at face value, but to subject evidence challenging one's views to special scrutiny, seeking flaws or weaknesses in these unwelcome facts. This tendency can easily be documented in trials. In one study, participants were first exposed to a newspaper article that created a bias about a particular murder trial. These pretend "jurors" were then presented with the trial evidence and had to evaluate how persuasive each bit of evidence was. The results showed a clear effect of the newspaper article: Evidence consistent with the (biased) pretrial publicity was seen as more compelling; evidence inconsistent with the publicity was seen as less compelling. And, of course, this effect fed on itself. Each bit of evidence that the "jurors" heard was filtered through their confirmation bias, so the evidence seemed particularly persuasive if it favored the view the "jurors" held already. This led the "jurors" to be more confident that their view was, in fact, correct. (After all, the evidence—as they interpreted it—did seem to favor that view.) This now-stronger view, in turn, amplified the confirmation bias, which colored how the "jurors" interpreted the next bit of evidence. Thus, around and around we go—with confirmation bias coloring how the evidence is interpreted, which strengthens the "jurors'" belief, which creates more confirmation bias, which colors how later evidence is interpreted, which further strengthens the belief.

Does this pattern matter? Surely it does: In this study, the pretrial publicity did have a powerful effect on the "jurors'" final verdict. Let's be clear, though, that the publicity did not influence the verdict directly. Odds are good that the "jurors" weren't thinking of the publicity at all when they voted "guilty" or "not guilty." Instead, their verdicts were based (as they should be) on the participants' evaluation of the trial evidence. The problem, though, is that this evaluation of the evidence was itself powerfully shaped by the pretrial publicity, via the mechanisms we have just described.

In light of these results, we might worry that the courts' protections against juror bias may not be adequate. In some trials, for example, jurors are merely asked: "Can you set aside any personal beliefs or knowledge you have obtained outside the court and decide this case solely on the evidence you hear from the witness stand?" Such questions seem a thin shield against juror prejudice. As one concern, jurors *might not know* whether they'll be able to set aside their prejudices. They might not realize, in other words, that they are vulnerable to belief bias or confirmation bias, and so they might overestimate their ability to overcome these effects. In a related point, jurors might be determined to vote, in the jury room, based only on what they heard during the trial. As we have now seen, though, that's no protection at all from prior prejudice.

Laboratory results tell us that belief bias and confirmation bias are powerful effects that often work in a fashion that is completely unconscious. This strongly suggests that the courts need to seek more powerful means of avoiding these influences in order to ensure each defendant a fair and unbiased trial. Possible solutions include stricter screening of jurors, and procedures that would make it easier to change a trial's location. In any case, it seems clear that stronger precautions are needed than those currently in place.

For more on this topic

Hope, L., Memon, A., & McGeorge, P. (2004). Understanding pretrial publicity: Predecisional distortion of evidence by mock jurors. *Journal of Experimental Psychology: Applied, 10*, 111–119.

FOR DISCUSSION

Often research data force us to rethink policy issues. For example, democratic governments are usually committed to the principle of freedom of the press, so that newspapers and television are allowed to report on whatever topics they choose. At the same time, though, it appears that some forms of news coverage—namely, pretrial publicity—can be damaging to the judicial process. How should we think about this apparent conflict between the desirability of a free press and the desirability of a fair legal system?

Setting these policy issues to the side, though, the psychological question remains: What might we do to provide remedies for the influence of pretrial publicity? Bear in mind that changing the location of a trial—to some other county or some other state—is often quite expensive. Bear in mind that selecting just those jurors who don't follow the news at all might produce a jury that's not representative of the community. In light of these concerns, what should we do about the effects of pretrial publicity?

Solving Problems

Demonstrations

14.1   Analogies

Analogies are a powerful help in solving problems, but they are also an excellent way to convey new information. Imagine that you're a teacher, trying to explain some points about astronomy. Which of the following explanations do you think would be more effective?

Literal Version

Collapsing stars spin faster and faster as they fold in on themselves and their size decreases. This phenomenon of spinning faster as the star's size shrinks occurs because of a principle called "conservation of angular momentum."

Analogy Version

Collapsing stars spin faster as their size shrinks. Stars are thus like ice-skaters, who pirouette faster as they pull in their arms. Both stars and skaters operate by a principle called "conservation of angular momentum."

Which version of the explanation would make it easier for students to answer a question like the following one?

What would happen if a star "expanded" instead of collapsing?

    a. Its rate of rotation would increase.

    b. Its rate of rotation would decrease.

    c. Its orbital speed would increase.

    d. Its orbital speed would decrease.

Does your intuition tell you the analogy version would be better as a teaching tool? If so, then your intuitions are in line with the data! Participants in one study were

131

presented with materials just like these, in either a literal or an analogy version. Later, they were asked questions about these materials, and those instructed via analogy reliably did better. Do you think your teachers make effective use of analogy? Can you think of ways they can improve their use of analogy?

Demonstration adapted from: Donnelly, C., & McDaniel, M. (1993). Use of analogy in learning scientific concepts. *Journal of Experimental Psychology: Learning, Memory and Cognition, 19*(4), 975–987. Copyright © 1993 by the American Psychological Association. Adapted with permission. *Also,* Donnelly, C., & McDaniel, M. (2000). Analogy with knowledgeable learners: When analogy confers benefits and exacts costs. *Psychonomic Bulletin & Review, 7,* 537–543.

14.2   Incubation

Many people believe that an "incubation" period aids problem-solving. In other words, spending time *away from the problem* helps you to find the solution, because, during the time away, you are unconsciously continuing to work on the problem.

Is this belief warranted—an accurate reflection of how problem-solving truly proceeds? To find out, psychologists study problem-solving in the lab, using problems like these.

Each of the figures shown here represents a familiar word or phrase. Can you decipher them? To get you started, the first figure represents the common phrase "reading between the lines."

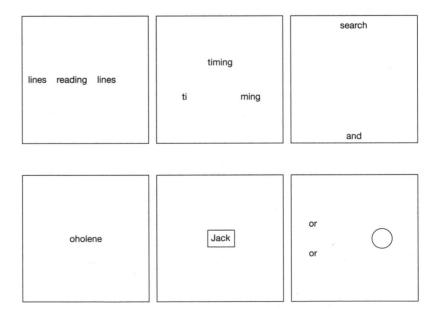

Puzzles like these are sometimes used in laboratory explorations of problem-solving, including studies of incubation. In one study, for some of the figures shown here, a helpful clue was provided (thus, the fourth picture here might be accompanied by the word "nothing"). For other figures, the clue was actually misleading (e.g., the third picture here might be accompanied by the clue "chemical").

It turns out that finding the solutions to these puzzles was more likely if participants tried the problem, then took a break, then returned to the problem. However, the explanation for this probably does not involve "unconscious problem-solving" that took place during the break. Instead, the break helped simply because it allowed the participants to lose track of the bad strategies they'd been trying so far, and this in turn allowed the participants to get a fresh start on the problem when they returned to it after the break. This was particularly evident in the puzzles that were presented with misleading cues: Spending a little time away from the puzzle allowed participants to forget the misleading clue, and so they were no longer misled and thus more likely to solve the puzzle.

The solutions, by the way, are "reading between the lines," "split-second timing," "search high and low," "hole in one," "jack in the box," and "double or nothing." If you'd like to try a few more, try the Frame Games page on syndicated puzzle columnist Terry Stickels's website: www.terrystickels.com/frame=games/.

Demonstration adapted from: Smith, S., & Blankenship, S. (1989). Incubation effects. *Bulletin of the Psychonomic Society, 27*, 311–314. *Also,* Smith, S., & Blankenship, S. (1991). Incubation and the persistence of fixation in problem solving. *American Journal of Psychology, 104*, 61–87. *Also,* Vul, E., & Pashler, H. (2007). Incubation benefits only after people have been misdirected. *Memory and Cognition, 35*, 701–710.

14.3   Verbalization and Problem-Solving

Research on problem-solving has attempted to determine what factors *help* problem-solving (making it faster or more effective) and what factors *hinder* problem-solving. Some of these factors are surprising.

You'll need a clock or timer for this one. Read the first problem below, and give yourself 2 minutes to find the solution. If you haven't found the solution in this time, take a break for 90 seconds; during those 90 seconds, turn away from the problem and try to say out loud, in as much detail as possible, everything you can remember about how you have been trying to solve the problem. Give information about your approach, your strategies, any solutions you tried, and so on. Then go back and try working on the problem for another 2 minutes.

Then do the same for the next problem—2 minutes of trying a solution, 90 seconds of describing out loud everything you can remember about how you have been trying to solve the problem, and then another 2 minutes of working on the problem.

Problem 1: The drawing below shows ten pennies. Can you make the triangle point downward by moving only three of the pennies?

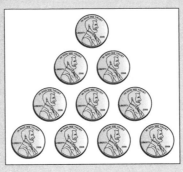

Problem 2: Nine pigs are kept together in a square pen. Build two more square enclosures that will isolate each pig, so that each is in a pen all by itself.

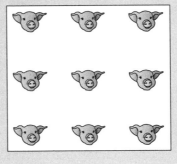

Do you think the time spent describing your efforts so far *helped you*, perhaps by allowing you to organize your thinking, or *hurt you*? In fact, in several studies this sort of "time off, to describe your efforts so far" makes it *less likely* that people will solve these problems. In one study, participants solved 36% of the problems if they had verbalized their efforts so far, but 46% of the problems if they didn't go through the verbalization step. Does this fit with your experience?

Why does verbalization interfere with this form of problem-solving? One likely explanation is that verbalization focuses the problem-solver's attention on the efforts so far, which may make it more difficult to abandon those efforts and try new approaches. The verbalization can also focus the problem-solver's attention on the sorts of strategies that are deliberate, conscious, and easily described in words, which may interfere with strategies that are not deliberate, unconscious, and not easily articulated. In all cases, though, the pattern makes it clear that sometimes "thinking out loud" and trying to communicate your ideas to others can actually be counterproductive! Exactly why this is, and what this implies about problem-solving, is a topic in need of further research.

For solutions to the two problems, turn the page.

Here are the solutions.

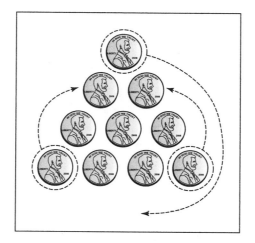

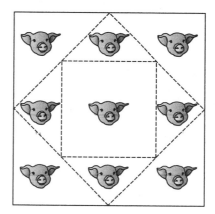

Demonstration adapted from: Schooler, J., Ohlsson, S. & Brooks, K. (1993). Thoughts beyond words: When language overshadows insight. *Journal of Experimental Psychology: General, 122,* 166–183.

Applying Cognitive Psychology

Research Methods: Defining the Dependent Variable

In our first Research Methods essay, we discussed the importance of testable hypotheses—that is, hypotheses that are framed in a way that makes it clear what evidence will fit them and what evidence will not. Sometimes, though, it's not obvious how to phrase a hypothesis in testable terms. For example, in Chapter 14 of the textbook we discuss research on creativity, and within this research investigators often offer hypotheses about the factors that might foster creativity or might undermine it. Thus, one hypothesis might be: "When working on a problem, an interruption (to allow incubation) promotes creativity." To test this hypothesis, we would have to specify what counts as an interruption (5 minutes of working on something else? an hour?). But then we'd also need some way to measure creativity; otherwise, we couldn't tell if the interruption was beneficial or not.

For this hypothesis, creativity is the *dependent variable*—that is, the measurement that, according to our hypothesis, might "depend on" the thing being manipulated. The presence or absence of an interruption would be the *independent variable*—the factor that, according to our hypothesis, influences the dependent variable.

In many studies, it's easy to assess the dependent variable. For example, consider this hypothesis: "Context reinstatement improves memory accuracy." Here the dependent variable is accuracy, and this is simple to check—for example, by counting up the number of correct answers on a memory test. In this way, we would easily know whether a result confirmed the hypothesis or not. Likewise, consider this hypothesis: "Implicit memories can speed up performance on a lexical decision task." Here the dependent variable is response time; again, it is simple to measure, allowing a straightforward test of the hypothesis.

The situation is different, though, for our hypothesis about interruptions and creativity. In this case, people might disagree about whether a particular problem solution (or poem, or painting, or argument) is creative or not. This will make it difficult to test our hypothesis.

Psychologists generally solve this problem by recruiting a panel of judges to assess the dependent variable. In our example, the judges would review each participant's response and evaluate how creative it was, perhaps on a scale from 1 to 5. By using a panel of judges rather than just one, we can check directly on whether different judges have different ideas about what creativity is. More specifically, we can calculate the *interrater reliability* among the judges—the degree to which they agree with each other in their assessments. If they disagree with each other, then it would appear that the assessment of creativity really is a subjective matter and cannot be a basis for testing hypotheses. In that case, scientific research on this issue may not be possible. But if the judges do agree to a reasonable extent—if the interrater reliability is high—then we can be confident that their assessments are neither arbitrary nor idiosyncratic, and so they can be used for testing hypotheses.

Notice, ironically, that this way of proceeding doesn't require us to have a precise definition of creativity. Of course, a definition would be very useful since (among other benefits) it would allow us to give the judges on our panel relatively specific instructions. Even without a definition, though, we can just ask the judges to rely on their own sense of what's creative. If we find out that they largely agree in their assessments, then we can use these assessments as our measurement of whatever it is that people intuitively label as "creativity." This isn't ideal; we'd prefer to get beyond this intuitive notion. But having a systematic, nonidiosyncratic consensus measurement at least allows our research to get off the ground.

In the same way, consider this hypothesis: "College education improves the quality of critical thinking." Or: "Time pressure increases the likelihood that people will offer implausible problem solutions." These hypotheses, too, involve complex dependent variables, and they might also require a panel of judges to obtain measurements we can take seriously. But by using these panels, we can measure things that seem at the outset to be unmeasurable, and in that way we appreciably broaden the range of hypotheses we can test.

FOR DISCUSSION

A number of different television shows have centered on talent competitions: Who is the best singer? The best dancer? The funniest stand-up comedian? Who should be the next American idol? In some cases, these television shows let the *viewers* decide: People call in and vote for their favorite singer or dancer or comic. For some shows, people can call as many times as they wish and cast as many votes as they want to. For these shows, the phone lines are often jammed when the time comes to vote, and so people who are less persistent (less willing to dial and redial and redial) end up not voting; only the persistent viewers vote. Is this a reasonable way to judge talent? Using the points made in this essay (concerned with how researchers assess a dependent variable) and

the points made in previous essays (e.g., the Research Methods essay on systematic data collection for Chapter 12), can you evaluate this voting procedure as a means of seeking to find the best singer or the best dancer?

On other TV shows, things run differently: A *panel* of (supposedly expert) judges does the voting—and decides who stays on the show and who goes away. Is this a reasonable way to judge talent?

Finally, on still other shows, there is just *one judge*—one expert chef, for example, who decides which of the contestants is the worst cook that week and so is removed from the show. Is this a reasonable way to judge talent?

Cognitive Psychology and Education:
Making Better Problem Solvers

Chapter 14 is concerned directly with the limitations on problem-solving and how people can overcome those limitations. In this essay, we will draw together some of the lessons that are evident in the chapter.

First, it is useful to note that people often approach problems with relatively primitive strategies, such as hill-climbing. This strategy often works—but not if a problem requires that during the solution you temporarily move *away* from the goal, in order to reach a different position from which you can more effectively move *toward* the goal. This is an important fact to keep in mind, because people routinely get bogged down in their problem-solving when they hit a problem that requires them to move "backward" for a while, in order to move forward again.

Similarly, it is useful to keep in mind that some problems are easier to solve by moving from the goal state to the starting state, rather than the other way around. Even experts resort to this sort of working backward if the problem is one they don't immediately recognize. Thus, problem-solvers, in general, are well advised to keep this option in mind.

Next, the chapter emphasizes the point that even though analogies are enormously useful, people often fail to use them. Students can diminish this difficulty, however, in a variety of ways. Research indicates that analogy use is more common if you've seen multiple analogues in the past, and not just one or two. Presumably, this exposure to multiple examples encourages you to think about what the examples have in common; this in turn will lead you to think about the examples' underlying dynamic, rather than their superficial features—which is exactly the right path toward promoting analogy use. This is, by the way, why homework exercises are often useful. The exercises sometimes seem redundant, but the redundancy turns out to have a function.

Likewise, you can improve your problem-solving by trying explicitly to compare problems to each other and asking what they have in common. This, too, promotes attention to the problems' underlying dynamic, increasing the likelihood of the problems being useful as the basis for analogies later on.

Still related, you can ask yourself what makes a problem's solution successful. One way to do this is to explain the solution to a friend—or even just to think about explaining it to a friend. The rationale here is a familiar one: In thinking about why the solution gets the job done, you put your attention on the problem's dynamic rather than on its surface features, and that's what leads to better problem-solving.

Then, as one final (but similar) step, it is sometimes helpful to divide a problem solution into parts and to seek a meaningful label for each part. The labels will themselves make the solution easier to remember; the exercise of dividing a larger problem into subproblems is also, on its own, helpful in tackling many problems. In addition, the search for—and the finding of—good descriptive labels will once again showcase why and how the problem solution is effective.

Each of these steps will require a bit more effort on your part and a bit more thought about the exercises you encounter during training—whether it's training in how to solve a homework assignment for a physics class, or training in how to assemble a good argument for a literature class, or training in how to design a compelling experiment for a psychology class. But the effort is likely to pay off. It's no surprise that analogies can be enormously useful. What is surprising is how often people overlook potential analogies—and thereby handicap their own problem-solving. The techniques described here will go some distance toward remedying this situation.

Cognitive Psychology and the Law:
Problem-Solving in the Courts

In many trials, judge and jury are trying to make a straightforward decision: The defendant is either innocent or guilty; the lawsuit should be decided for the plaintiff or for the defendant. These decisions can be enormously difficult, but at least the task is clear: Gather and evaluate the evidence; make a choice between two outcomes.

In other cases, though, the court's role is different. The court has a goal and must figure out how to reach the goal. In a divorce case, for example, the goal is to reach a settlement that is fair for both husband and wife; if the couple has dependent children, the goal must also include a living arrangement for the children that will be sensitive to their needs. Likewise, in a bankruptcy case the goal is to arrive at a distribution of resources that is fair for everyone.

These cases suggest that we should sometimes think of the courts as engaged in problem-solving, rather than decision-making. As the textbook chapter describes, problem-solving begins with an initial state (the circumstances you are in right now) and a goal state (the circumstances you hope to reach). The task is to find some path that will lead you from the former to the latter. In many court cases, the problem is an *ill-defined* one: We know roughly what the goal state will involve (namely, a solution that is fair for all parties concerned), but the specifics of the goal state are far from clear.

In addition, some people argue that solutions to legal disputes should, as much as possible, promote the health and well-being of all parties involved. This emphasis, sometimes called "therapeutic jurisprudence," adds another goal in our search for a problem solution.

The search for these solutions can be difficult. The judge (or other mediator) needs to be fair and pragmatic but often also needs to be insightful, creative, and perhaps even wise. How can we help people to find these King Solomon–like solutions? Legal scholars, therapists, social workers, and others have all offered their advice, but it also seems plausible that we might gain some insights from the study of problem-solving.

As an illustration, many courtroom settlements can be guided by *analogy*. A judge, for example, might find an equitable resolution for a child-custody dispute by drawing an analogy from a previously decided case. Likewise, a mediator might find a fair divorce or bankruptcy settlement by appealing to some suitable analogy. Of course, judges already use analogies; this is built into the idea that settlements must be guided by appropriate legal *precedents*. But we know that in general people often fail to find and use appropriate analogies, and also that there are steps we can take to promote analogy use. It seems likely, therefore, that we can use these steps to help legal decision-makers become better problem-solvers and, in that fashion, provide real benefit for the criminal justice system. However, little research investigates this specific point, and cognitive psychology's potential contribution to this important area is so far underexplored. It is therefore an area that we can recommend to students and to colleagues as being in need of research and further development.

For more on this topic

Winick, B. J. (1998). Sex offender law in the 1990s: A therapeutic jurisprudence analysis. *Psychology, Public Policy, and Law, 4,* 505–570.

Winick, B. J., & Wexler, D. B. (2003). *Judging in a therapeutic key: Therapeutic jurisprudence and the courts.* Durham, NC: Carolina Academic Press.

FOR DISCUSSION

What sorts of training would you propose to teach judges and mediators how to be better problem-solvers? What sorts of materials would you expose them to? What perspective or attitude would you encourage them to bring to this training material?

In thinking this through, bear in mind that research provides some guidance on these issues—including the sort of training materials that promote analogy use, as well as the attitudes during training that make subsequent analogy use more likely.

CHAPTER 15

Conscious Thought, Unconscious Thought

Demonstrations

15.1   Practice and the Cognitive Unconscious

Chapter 15 describes just how much we can accomplish via the cognitive unconscious, so that we can perform complex, sophisticated actions on "autopilot." One path toward placing a task on autopilot is, quite simply, practice: With sufficient practice, we can achieve difficult feats without giving them any thought at all.

As one way to document this, take a piece of paper and write down step-by-step instructions for *how to tie your shoes*. Assume that the person you're writing for has the basic vocabulary (and so knows what a "lace" is, what "left" and "right" mean, what a "loop" or a "cross" is, and so on). But assume this person has never tied shoes before and will need complete, detailed instructions.

Once you have done this, recruit a friend. Give him or her an untied shoe to work with, and then read your instructions out loud, one sentence at a time. Ask your friend to follow your instructions exactly. Make sure that your friend doesn't just rely on his or her own knowledge; instead, your friend must do exactly what you say in your instructions—no more and no less!

Will the shoe end up tied? Odds are good that it will not, and you're likely to end up with your friend's arms tied in knots, and not the laces.

Of course, you know perfectly well how to tie your shoes; you do it every day. But the sequence of steps is automatic and something you barely think about. Indeed, this demonstration suggests that even when you *want* to think about this everyday activity, you can't—the steps are so automatic that they've become largely inaccessible to your conscious thinking.

15.2   The Quality of Consciousness

One of the remarkable things about consciousness is that people seem to differ from each other in the quality of their consciousness. Of course, people think different things and have different ideas and beliefs. What's amazing, though, is that people differ in the very nature of their thoughts—so that some people routinely have experiences that are utterly foreign to other individuals. To make this concrete, ask the following questions of several friends:

Imagine a girl carrying an umbrella. Can you see her in your mind's eye? Now, is the umbrella open or closed? Is it on her shoulder or held in front of her? Is she facing you or standing in profile? What is she wearing? What color is her jacket, or is she not wearing a jacket? What color are her boots? What's in the background behind the girl?

What sorts of responses do you get from your friends? It's inevitable that the answers will differ in the details. (Some people might imagine a blue jacket; others might imagine yellow; and so on.) But what's striking is that your friends' answers will probably indicate that they are having different *types* of experiences. At one extreme, some of your friends are likely to have an immensely detailed visual picture and will give you very fast and complete answers to every question. In describing their image, they'll sound as if they were effortlessly reading off information from an *actual* picture, not a mental picture.

At the other extreme, though, some of your friends may describe a very different experience. When you ask them about the umbrella, they'll say something like: "I wasn't thinking about the umbrella's position until you mentioned it." When you ask them about colors, they may say: "What I'm thinking isn't in color *or* in black and white; it's just a thought, and I don't have a sense of it being in any way colored or not colored." In short, they may describe an experience that's not in any fashion picturelike. Remarkably, they may insist that they *never* have picturelike inner experiences and never feel as though they can see a "mental picture" with their "mind's eye." Surely, they will have heard these (often-used) phrases, but they will think of them as loose metaphors and will insist that "mental seeing" doesn't feel in any fashion like "actual seeing." (You may need to question several friends until you find someone at this extreme.)

What should we make of these variations? Is it possible that some people routinely have conscious experiences ("mental pictures") that are totally different from the types of conscious experiences that other people have? Do these differences from one person to the next matter—for what they can do or what they can do easily? If so, this becomes a powerful argument that the experience of being conscious really does matter—does change how we act, what we say, and how we think or feel.

Applying Cognitive Psychology

Research Methods: Introspection

In Chapter 1, we discussed some of the limits on introspection as a research tool; in fact, our discussion throughout the textbook has rarely relied on introspective evidence. This is because, as one concern, introspection relies on what people remember about their own mental processes, and we cannot count on these memories being reliable. In addition, introspections are usually reported verbally: The person uses words to describe what happened in his or her own mind. But as we discussed in Chapter 11, some of our thoughts are nonverbal in content and may not be captured adequately by a verbal description.

As a further problem, introspection assumes that our mental states are "visible" to us, so that they can be introspected. As Chapter 15 describes, however, a great deal of our mental activity goes on outside of awareness, and so it is, by its very nature, "invisible"—to introspection. It might seem, therefore, that introspection must fail as a basis for psychological research.

Let's be careful, though, not to overstate these claims, because unmistakably introspective reports sometimes do have value. For example, in Chapter 14 we relied on problem-solving protocols (descriptions of someone's thought processes while working on a problem, produced by simply asking the person to "think out loud") as a basis for discovering some of the strategies people use in problem-solving. In Chapter 11, we noted that there are complexities attached to someone's introspective reports about the vividness of his or her own images, but we argued that these vividness reports are nonetheless an important source of data about images. (Also see Demonstration 15.2, p. 142.) And in Chapter 6, we explored the nature of implicit memories; an important source of data there was people's introspective reports about whether a stimulus "felt familiar" or not.

How can we reconcile these uses of introspective data with the concerns we've raised about this type of data? The answer lies in research designed to ask whether each type of introspection can be taken seriously or not. Thus, if problem-solving protocols suggest that people use certain strategies, we can seek other evidence to confirm (or disconfirm) this introspection. We can ask, for example, whether people make the sort of errors that we'd expect if they are, in fact, using the strategies suggested by the protocols. We can ask if people have trouble with problems they can't solve via these strategies, and so on. In this way, we can check on the introspections and thus find out if the protocols provide useful evidence for us.

Likewise, in Chapter 11 we discussed some of the evidence indicating that reports of image vividness do have value, because we can use these reports as a basis both for predicting how well people will do in certain tasks and for predicting which people will show particularly strong activation in the visual cortex while engaged in visual imagery. So here, too, we can document the value of the introspective evidence, even if, in general, we have powerful reasons to be skeptical about introspections.

Notice, then, that introspection is neither wholly worthless nor wonderfully reliable. Instead, introspections can provide us with fabulous clues about what's going on in someone's mind—but we then need to find other means of checking on those clues to determine if they are misleading us or not. But let's also note that introspection is not unique in this regard. Any research tool must prove its worth—by means of data that in one fashion or another validate the results obtained with that tool. In this way, we use our research methods to build our science, but we also use our science to check on and, where possible, refine our research methods.

For more on this topic

Stone, A., Turkkan, J., Bachrach, C., Jobe, J., Kurtzman, H., & Cain, V. (Eds.), 2000. *The science of self-report: Implications for research and practice.* Mahwah, NJ: Erlbaum.

FOR DISCUSSION

In many settings, we are asked to introspect: A close friend asks you, "Do you love me?" A teacher asks, "Why did you choose that answer?" A marketing survey asks, "Why did you decide to buy a Japanese car rather than one from Europe or the United States?" A therapist asks, "Why do you think your roommate annoys you so much?" Or you ask yourself, "Why can't I keep my attention focused on my studies?" or "What do I really want to major in?"

In light of the points raised in this essay about introspection, and in light of the points raised in the text-book chapter, how much confidence should we have in your ability to answer these questions accurately and completely? And if your answers might be inaccurate or incomplete, does that mean we should stop asking these questions? In thinking about these points, be alert to the fact that your response may depend on exactly what you're being asked to introspect about and who is doing the asking. You might also want to consider the possibility that introspections—even if incomplete or inaccurate—might nonetheless be useful for many purposes.

Cognitive Psychology and Education: Mindfulness

As the textbook chapter discusses, we are able to accomplish a great deal through unconscious processing, and in many ways *this is a good thing.* With no attention paid to the low-level details of a task, and with no thought given to the processes needed for the task, we are able to focus our attention instead on other priorities—our broader goals or the products (the ideas, the memories, the beliefs) resulting from these unconscious, unnoticed processes.

The chapter also makes it clear, though, that there is a cost associated with these benefits. It is is helpful that we don't have to pay attention to most mental processes; this frees us to pay attention to other things instead. But at the same time, we end up being less able to *control* our own mental processes and also *less aware* of why we ultimately believe what we believe, perceive what we perceive, feel what we feel. With this, we end up more likely to rely on habit or routine, and more vulnerable to the pressures or cues built into the situations we encounter. We're also more likely to be influenced by chance associations and by the relatively primitive thought processes that, in Chapter 12, we referred to as System 1 thinking.

It's not surprising, therefore, that some people urge us to be more *mindful* of our actions and, in general, to seek a state of mindfulness. Sports coaches, piano teachers, writing instructors, and many others all urge us to "pay attention" to what we're doing—on the sports field, at the piano, at the word processor—with the clear notion that by paying attention we'll be able to rise above old habits and adjust our performance in one fashion or another. In the same spirit, instructors sometimes complain about their students performing a task in a "mechanical" fashion or "on auto-pilot," with the broad suggestion that a thoughtful, more mindful performance would be better—more alert to the circumstances, better tuned to the situation. Likewise, commonsense wisdom urges us to "Look before you leap" or sometimes just to "Think!"—apparently based on the idea that some forethought, or some thought during an action, might help us to be more aware of, and therefore wiser about, what we are doing.

These various suggestions—all celebrating the advantages of mindfulness—fit well with the argument that unconscious processes tend to be habitual, inflexible, and too rigidly controlled by situational cues or prior patterns. But how should you use this information? How should you try to be more mindful? You might start by asking yourself: "What is my usual practice in taking notes in class? What is my usual strategy when the time comes to prepare for an exam? What does the rhythm of my typical day look like?" In each case, you might pause to ask whether these practices and strategies developed for good reasons or simply out of habit. In each case, you might ask yourself whether, on reflection, you might want to modify your practices to take advantage of some of the suggestions you've read about in these essays or found in other sources. In these ways, some thoughtful, mindful, and *conscious* reflection on your thoughts and behaviors may lead you to some improvements in how you think, what you think, and how you act.

For more on this topic

Brown, K., Ryan, M., & Creswell, J. (2007). Mindfulness: Theoretical foundations and evidence for its salutary effects. *Psychological Inquiry, 18*, 211–237.

Cognitive Psychology and the Law:
Unconscious Thinking

Chapter 15 of the textbook argues that much of our thinking goes on unconsciously, and this fact turns out to have important implications for the legal system. In many trials, for example, the judge knows that jurors have been exposed to prejudicial pre-trial publicity. The judge may ask the jurors, therefore, whether they think they'll be able to set aside what they've heard prior to the trial and decide a verdict based only on the trial evidence. But how accurately can the jurors answer this question? Can the jurors forecast what they'll be influenced by? Then, at the time of the verdict, will the jurors know whether they were influenced by the pretrial publicity? Research on the cognitive unconscious suggests pessimistic answers to these questions—because the relevant influences were all unconscious, and so not something the jurors could ever assess.

Similar concerns apply to the trial's witnesses. Imagine, for example, that the police show you six photographs and ask you to pick out the man who robbed you. After you make your choice, the police officer smiles and says, "Yes, that's who we suspected. By the way, how certain are you in your selection?" Then the officer asks some additional questions: "How good a view did you get of the perpetrator? How far away was the perpetrator? For how many seconds was the perpetrator in view?"

In this situation, notice that you received a bit of confirming feedback right after the identification ("Yes, that's who we suspected"), and this has a powerful influence. As we mentioned in Chapter 7, research participants given this sort of feedback report that they are more confident in their choice, compared with participants not given feedback. Participants given this feedback also end up remembering that they paid closer attention, had a better view, and were able to see more of the perpetrator's face, in comparison to people not given this feedback. Of course, these recollections are mistaken—because, in the experiments, the feedback and no-feedback groups got exactly the same view and could see exactly the same details.

Why does feedback have these effects? It is as if research participants were saying to themselves, "I guess I can set my doubts to the side, because the officer told me that I did get it right. With my doubts now suspended, I suppose I can say that I'm certain. And since I apparently chose the right guy, I guess I must have gotten a good view, been standing close enough, and so on. Otherwise, I'd have no explanation for why I made the right choice and am so confident in my choice."

This certainly sounds as if participants are drawing inferences from the feedback and reaching conclusions about what they did or didn't see. But such reasoning happens unconsciously. Participants are aware only of the *product* that results from these steps: a certain level of confidence in their identification, and a set of recollections about the event. They are entirely unaware of the *process* that led to these products. And as the chapter describes, there is nothing unusual or exotic about this example. Instead, this is the way cognition works in general—with most of our thought process hidden from view.

In these and other ways, research on the cognitive unconscious suggests that jurors and witnesses do *not* know their own minds, and this point raises serious questions about some courtroom and police procedures. For example, I've testified in some trials about these feedback effects and how feedback right after an identification can influence a witness. In rebuttal, the court re-called the witness to the stand and asked him directly: "Were you influenced in any way by the feedback you received?" The witness confidently said no, and his denial was apparently quite persuasive to the jury. However, the jury probably got this wrong, because the witness's denial is in fact of little value. The denial simply tells us that the witness wasn't *consciously* influenced by the feedback, but that doesn't mean that the witness was immune to the feedback.

It seems likely, then, that we'll need to adjust some of our procedures—and perhaps, in the process, we'll need to take multiple steps to persuade jurors on these points, so that they'll be more sophisticated in their thinking about what's conscious and what's not. This would, we hope, help both witnesses and jurors to think more accurately about the nature of—and the sources of—their own thoughts, memories, and judgments.

For more on this topic

Bradfield, A., et al. (2002). The damaging effect of confirming feedback on the relation between eyewitness certainty and identification accuracy. *Journal of Applied Psychology, 87,* 112–120.

Wells, G. L., Olson, E. A., & Charman, S. (2002). The confidence of eyewitnesses in their identifications from lineups. *Current Directions in Psychological Science, 11,* 151–154.

FOR DISCUSSION

Judges will not allow experts to testify in a trial if their testimony would only rehash points that the jury already understands. On this point, expert testimony about *memory* is often forbidden, with the judge arguing something like this: "We all have memories. We all use our memories all the time. We all therefore have a wonderful opportunity, across our lives, to learn how memories work. Therefore, we don't need an expert to testify on these points; instead, anything the expert might offer is likely to be just a matter of common sense—and thus already known to the jury."

Is this skepticism about memory research justified? Does this research just echo common sense? You might think about this point with a focus on the postidentification feedback effect: The witness is convinced that his or her memories of the past come from one source, but research indicates that these "memories" aren't memories at all; they are instead after-the-fact inferences based on the feedback the witness has received. Are there other examples of unconscious processes, influencing memory, that also undermine our (common-sense) beliefs about how memory functions and how much faith we can put in our memories?